JOHN HENRIK CLARKE

The Early Years

Barbara Eleanor Adams

Published by
United Brothers and Sisters Comunications
1040-D Settlers Landing Road
Hampton, Virginia 23669
1-804-723-2696

FIRST EDITION ● FIRST PRINTING

SEPTEMBER, 1992

Cover Design by Cloice Fannin
Front Cover Picture by Anthony Barboza
Back Cover Picture by Allen Morgan
Picture Section Researched, Edited and Arranged by
Barbara Eleanor Adams
Special Consultant: Mark W. Payne

ISBN#1-56411-040-0   Y.B.B.G#0036

Printed in the U. S. A. by
United Brothers and Sisters
Printing and Graphics Unlimited
Compositor, Bessie "Khayruh" Bowser
P. O. Box 5368 ● Newport News, Virginia 23605
1-804-723-2696

Dedication

To my three wonderful children:

Wesley Adam Rose, Gyl-Maria Rose, and Timitra Nicole Rose whom I raised alone. You motivated me and were my inspiration to return to college to create a better life for you. Thank you for graduating from college and for being productive. You have made me very proud. I love you.

In order to retain the flavor of Dr. Clarke's unique form of peaking, the language remains in its original form, written in the first person, with limited editing. One should "read" this work with a musical ear, as one would listen to the voice of an African griot.

ACKNOWLEDGMENTS

My sincerest appreciation to Dr. Clarke who made thi book possible. This undertaking would not have beer possible without his generously giving me all the time needed by consenting to interviews, taping sessions anc numerous conversations. I will always be indebted to him for his confidence, trust and for taking a chance on my ability to record the early part of his life.

A very special thank you to Mary Clarke Hobbs anc children John and Lillie for their hospitality and friendship during many visits to Columbus. I am especially grateful to Mary for family pictures and her review of the Clarke history with me.

Accessibility to Dr. Clarke would not have been possible or so frequent, if not for the cooperation of Anna Swanston, Dr. Clarke's wonderful assistant. I must thank her for her guidance, kindness, and gentle manner always stressing the importance of patience.

For guidance, advice, assistance or encouragement on the project, I would like to thank: Marcia L. Tyler, my assistant; Jaffer Kassimali, Renita Carter and Morton Hall; Deborah Taylor for her skillful editing talents; Tilden J. LeMelle, Ph.D., and Beth Meador, Esquire for agreeing to review the manuscript.

To my friends Claudia J. Hurst and Mark W. Payne, I thank them for their support. Claudia's constant nudge over the years was a tremendous motivator. Mark, as special assistant to the project has been invaluable. He also accompanied me on my fourth trip to Columbus to photograph Dr. Clarke's family, former schools, friends and home.

There are friends who wished me well that I would also like to take the time to acknowledge. They are: Caren T. Allen-Sharpe, Ruth Ali, owner of the Bombay India Restaurant (where I spent many late evenings dreaming, planning and chatting), Laura Dell Battle, Don Gibbs, Uldeen Lee, H.L.M., Sr., Vida Damstrup-Nielsen, Lea Scott, Steve Stewart, Barbara Taylor, Ernestine Bell-Temple, Ms. "T" and Thomas Walker. For his interest and enthusiasm, I thank H. Khalif Khalifah, my publisher.

To my friends in Antigua and St. Thomas, Virgin Islands. I extend my thanks to them for their hospitality, welcoming me the many times I needed to get away to write near the blue Caribbean sea.

Thank-you children for your contributions, interest, suggestions, comments, assertiveness and criticism which were all well taken. Finally, I am deeply grateful to the celebrated photographer Anthony Barboza, for granting me the use of the now famous photograph of Dr. Clarke on the cover.

And, If I've failed to mention anyone who thinks they deserve mentioning, forgive me. It was merely an oversight and not intentional.

CONTENTS

FOREWORD

John Henrik Clarke was born in Union Springs, Alabama on January 1, 1915 to poor sharecropper farming parents. He grew up in Columbus, Georgia and came to New York in 1933 as a young man with the ambition of pursuing a career as a writer. From his early years, Dr. Clarke studied the history of the world, placing emphasis on the history of African people. He continued his studies by enrolling at New York University to major in history and world literature.

Dr. Clarke knew, at an early age, that he wanted to become an innovative classroom teacher. He told his father, who tried to understand, even though he had hoped his son would become a successful farmer with land of his own. However, Dr. Clarke's teaching career would start in the streets of New York City, using Harlem as his classroom, where he taught from a stepladder. Today he has attained the kind of success that would have made his father very proud.

As a writer of fiction, he has published over fifty short stories in this country and abroad. He has edited over twenty books, published four books during 1991, and is Professor Emeritus of African History in the Department of Black and Puerto Rican Studies of Hunter College, where he retired after a twenty-year teaching career.

I met Dr. Clarke for the first time when I enrolled in the African American History course that Hunter College offered two evenings a week in Harlem. He taught this class in the old Hotel Theresa located on 125th Street and Adam Clayton Powell Boulevard, then known as Seventh Avenue. His class was scheduled for this site because Dr. Clarke insisted on teaching at this location. He felt that if he was going to teach the history of our people, it should be taught in Harlem. The Hotel Theresa was the perfect place. His class at the Hotel Theresa was later discontinued and rescheduled for the Park Avenue Campus.

After the first class, I took every class to follow for the next five semesters. Each class was a new experience, I hung onto every word and was challenged to produce my best work each time. I earned A's for each class, but the grades did not come easy. His tests were lengthy and the take-home finals were worse, consisting of ten essay questions for which he expected ten full page answers intelligently written. While many of my classmates grumbled, I was completely motivated and relieved to learn that I could not only receive a decent grade for tests and term papers, but that I could still focus intellectually while raising my three young children.

I would sit in class mesmerized by his every word, eager to hear the scheduled weekly lecture on my ancestors. And as I listened, I often wondered why someone had not yet written a book on this great historian. It was several years later, with the undergraduate experience behind me, that I suggested to Dr. Clarke that a book should be written about him. He agreed, and while I sat amazed by his honesty, I somehow found the nerve to suggest myself as his biographer.

I cannot forget the positive feedback from the two people with whom I shared the initial news. The first reaction was from Dr. Tilden J. LeMelle,[1] then the Chairman of the Department of Black and Puerto Rican Studies of Hunter College. He was genuinely excited about the possibility of a book, and offered his assistance. His reaction gave me the confidence I needed at the time. But the best guidance I would receive on the project came from my friend Jaffer Kassimali, who was at Hunter then, still is, and is now the Acting Director of the Africana Studies Sequence in the Department of Black and Puerto Rican Studies. It was at his suggestion that I immediately began to read and examine many biographies and autobiographies for their layout, style, organization and design. His advice was priceless and I read as many books as I could get my hands on over the years while I wrote. I followed this advice until very recently. Among two of the numerous books that I found most influential were: *Maggie's American Dream*, written by James P. Comer, M.D.; and *Miles (The Autobiography)*, by Miles Davis and Quincy Troupe.

As I reminisce, I can say that, yes, I was intimidated by the idea. But with Dr. Clark's gentle manner and direction, I learned to relax while I recorded the important facts about his life. I remember the first taping very vividly. We

[1]Currently, the President of the University of the District of Columbia

started on June 25, 1980, in his home in Harlem, or Striver's Row and it was 90°. We proceeded in spite of the heat, and Dr. Clarke was chatty and brimming with information as we moved ahead.

In the beginning, he would suggest the starting point. He would often begin with his childhood but would invariably end up with Harlem in the 1930's. I am convinced that his favorite period was during the 1930's because it represented new awakenings, beginnings, and his arrival in New York. Because he is the consummate teacher, it carried over into our interviews and he would frequently announce how much we would cover, and where we would conclude for the day. Based on this routine, I quickly learned to arrive for the interviews with an outline or agenda which guided me and kept him focused on the topic for that day.

His ability to recall incidents that occurred fifty-nine or even seventy-three years ago astounded me. He tapped into my emotions when he spoke of his parents' collective efforts to feed the family on limited funds, and of his mother's conscientious effort to put aside a few cents for his education in spite of the family's ever-present poverty.

Countless hours of interviews were recorded concurrently with Dr. Clarke's busy lecture and world-wide travel schedule, and it was necessary to read and repeat these readings several times in order to tailor the chapter to his liking. However, *The Early Years* would not have been possible without his consent, his complete cooperation and inexhaustible patience, as evidenced by the following letter.

I am most appreciative and grateful to have been given this opportunity, since several educators and professional writers have recently approached Dr. Clarke, for his story, and there are rumors of several independent projects in progress.

I was overjoyed this past February, when after reading the completed manuscript to Dr. Clarke, he turned to me and said that I had done a good job, and he was pleased with what I wrote. I had followed his facial expression throughout the readings, as he listened carefully, and very intently to every word and detail. He remained composed and serene as I read. So by watching him closely, I already knew before he spoke that he was satisfied. His final comment was my greatest reward.

Barbara Eleanor Adams
Harlem, New York
February, 1992

April 27, 1987

Mrs. Barbara Adams
327 Convent Avenue
New York, New York 10031

Dear Mrs. Adams:

Dr. Joseph McLaren, Associate Professor at Mercy College has expressed an interest in assisting in the documentation of my contributions to world history and working on a biography of my life. I mentioned your name and your long years of work in this regard. I have forwarded to him your name and telephone and home address and you can expect a call from him relative to the biographical project.

Please feel free to make whatever arrangements you feel are fair and acceptable to you considering the fact that you have done most of the work at your personal expense. Have no hesitation in letting him know this.

Let me know how things work out.

Sincerely,

John H. Clarke

PART I

THE ORAL BIOGRAPHY

of

JOHN HENRIK CLARKE

as told to

BARBARA ELEANOR ADAMS

FIRST RECOLLECTIONS

When I was about three, close to it or in the neighborhood, my first recollections were discovering the many uncles and grandmas, and the many concerned faces around me because I fell off something. It was then that I discovered for the first time how much my family cared for children.

In this memory of many faces, one of my uncles took me to a well and put some water on my head, and my father kept saying "send the boy to me, send the boy to me," in a very anxious tone. My father said this to my Uncle Henry, part of whose name I had which I later changed to Henrik after I got to New York and was giving myself a college education. I became an admirer of the Scandinavian rebel playwright Henrik Ibsen, who was the first playwright who dared to mention something like the word syphilis on stage, and wrote *A Doll's House,* the first play about a woman's revolt against the treatment by her husband. In other words, he took up the social issues, and because I admired him, I changed the spelling of my name to the way he spelled his. I would legalize my name from Henry to Henrik when I entered the army, but growing up I was affectionately called Bubba by my immediate family to whom I am still known by this name.

We were sharecroppers and I wasn't conscious of the true poverty of a sharecropper family then, and wouldn't be conscious of it until later after the death of my mother, when my family was sent back to the farm where we were to remain about one year before my father chose a second wife. Then the full impact of the difficult life of a sharecropper family hit me, because we were literally driven off of our property, and forced to go live with an aunt through marriage, who was the wife of my Great Aunt's brother.

The difficulty of making a living on the farm was the key factor in why a lot of people left the farm to go to the next mill city (which was just across the Alabama State Line in Columbus, Georgia). We moved with the hope of making enough money to eventually buy the land rather than sharecrop the land. My father thought he would make enough money there for a better life, and ultimately come back to own some land so that he would become an independent farmer. It was basically a sharecropping community in which none of the Blacks of consequence owned any land.

John Henrik Clarke: The Early Years

I remember that our damaged roof was another reason we had to move in with another branch of the family. I remember the preparation to leave Alabama to go to the city. And so we moved into a house on the land owned by Ludi and Uncle Miller.

Uncle Miller had married a Mulatto named Ludi, whose father had died and left her land. She was light enough to pass for white, and was always threatening to disown us and go back to the white race. I kind of hoped she would but didn't know what we would do if she did because she was the only member of the family who had (I mean a lot of land), and we were living on her land now having been driven off of ours. She had a 7th grade education and later became the County Superintenent of Schools for the Colored. I think she probably married my uncle after some disappointment from another man.

In this cast of characters that I remember at the time, and will remember clearer later on, was my great grandmother, -- Ma Mary (she was my father's grandmother); my Aunt Liza, the midwife; and her brother.

During these first Molten Street years, my father was working in a brick yard tending kilns. What I remember most about these years was the the feeling of complete totality within a Black community, because everyone looked after each other. And with the memory of so many uncles, I later discovered that some of these uncles were not really relatives at all, and these are the ones who were most special to me. Now, the structure of our community developed and revolved around Macedonia Baptist Church. At the end of the street lived Reverend Chapman. We also lived at the end of the street near him, two doors away from Deacon Johnson, with Ms. Pearl Brown (Reverend Chapman's sister) on the other side. Ms. Pearl was the lady who started the rumor that I was such a little gentleman, because I was always tiping my hat. I then had to concentrate on becoming a little gentleman to keep from disappointing Ms. Pearl, which was quite a strain on me. When I think about it, I wish she had kept her mouth shut!

I remember the time when two of my mother's brothers visited and each gave me a nickel. For some reason, I put one in my piggy bank, to which they said, "ah, the boy is thrifty, he's going to save." Thereafter, each time they came to visit, both would give me a nickel, one of which I always saved. This habit seemed to start a prophesy about thriftiness.

Look, what people do sometimes is not what is prophesied for one to do. I had no sense of being thrifty. All I knew was that I had two nickels and didn't want to spend one, so I put the other one in the piggy bank. So now I have the reputation of being thrifty, and have to live up to this image I hadn't even given thought to Throughout most of my life, but especially my early life, have been fulfilling people's prophesies.

I remember some startling things that happened when lived on Molten Street, which made a strong impression on me as a youth. A lady decided that she wanted to preach and so she put a lamp out on her porch, and started conducting services. It was unheard of for a lady to preach in those days. Another thing I found fascinating were the tents that housed the medicine shows. They were found in the open lot in an area near Glade Road now called Cussetta Road.

It was also during my youth that a kind of dandy came to town, who wore good clothes, had a white steamer which was the Cadillac of the day, and carried a thousand dollar bill in his pocket. We called him the thousandaire. He never spent any money, because of course, he didn't want to break his thousand dollar bill. He conned everyone, especially the ladies. One day he miscalculated a turn in the road, and went into a ditch, whereupon white folks came to claim the car, which was their car anyway. They also took his clothes and everything else which he had borrowed from them while they were in Europe. He had, however, in that interval, given the townspeople a sense of grandeur with all his lies of travel and adventure.

I remember, too, the minstrel people singing the Old

John Henrik Clarke: The Early Years

West Indian Blues, with songs probably composed by Spencer Williams. These songs were sung as a tribute to the stick-to-it-ive-ness of Caribbean people. I had no consciousness of what a West Indian was, or was supposed to be. I really had no knowledge of Caribbean people at all until coming to New York City, and it wasn't until my arrival here that I immediately became active with people from the different islands, by visiting their respective social clubs. It was the time when the presence of Marcus Garvey was still in New York, because I heard the Marcus Garvey Blues for the first time.

MY FAMILY

My mother's name was Will Ella Mayes and my father's name was John. Both of them came from a little farm community in Union Sprins, Alabama. Most of the population in certain sections of Columbus, Georgia came from the same litle town called Union Springs.

Both of my grandmothers were named Mary. My father's mother was Mary and my great grandmother was Mary, but she was called Ma Mary and she was the oldest member of the family. She lived to be a hundred and eight, long enough to see her son, my father marry again. I even have a sister who we call Mary for the older women in the family, but her real name is Eddie Mae. She lives in Columbus and has four grown children; John Henry (who is named for me), Charlie Mae, Walter and Lillie.

I had many relatives on my father's side. My Great Aunt Sweet, my father's sister Aunt Bell who lived in Birmingham, and her daughter Louise. My father also had numerous brothers: Henry, Willie, and Bennie are the ones whose names I recall. All of these relatives have died.

My mother was a washer-woman who washed clothes for poor whites. There were other women in the neighborhood who had good bundles, but because my mother arrived after all the good bundles of the better class families were taken, she ended up washing for poor whites. They lived in North Highland, an area in Columbus, Georgia, which is also the place where, I am told, Carson McCullers, the writer once lived.

Now let me tell you what a bundle is. You worked for a rich white family, went to pick up the laundry, took it to your house, washed the clothes with your own soap powder, ironed them, then delivered the laundry back to the family. This is what is meant by a bundle. Now the better class of rich white folks gave you good bundles. They supplied their own detergent, and you didn't have to scrub their clothes as much, because they didn't get their clothes as dirty as the poor whites. Sometimes they delivered and picked up their clothes by car. Sometimes they tipped more than $1.00.

I used to go with my mother to pick up these bundles. She had a little red wagon which she used to take the laundry up and down the hills, and I would be in the wagon, on top of the bundles and she would pull both of us going home. Sometimes when she had different bundles which would net about $3.00, she would save about .50 cents a week. This money would be used eventually to educate her oldest son, -- me.

I remember that my mother was always feeding everyone, and that everyone came to the house to eat including the Chinese laundryman. I noticed that when my mother was feeding everyone, she would rarely sit down, to eat. She would eat standing up, and I did not know then that she was just eating the leavings from the bottom of the pot.

The first sickness of my mother began to set in, and think that she would still be alive today, if she had that same sickness, because it is now curable medically. You see, she had pellagra, and nobody dies from pellagra anymore. It's a diet deficiency, which has been totally wiped out.

My mother was ill intermittently when my brother Nathaniel was born, and because of her illness, he was taken away by a cousin Betty, when he was about two months old. We also called her Bebe. She was married to my cousin who worked for the railroad, and that meant something then -- to be married to a railroad worker, who was a person with a regular salary. My cousin Annie Bell was married to L.T. Taylor and he worked at the Round House. L.T., who brought home $54.00 every two weeks, was the richest man in the family.

With my mother's illness, and her subsequent death, we began to feel real poverty. I mean real poverty. I don't know how my mother could ward this off; however, whatever she did took more than just the few dollars she got from the bundles to keep up management of things.

My father was constantly out looking for additional work, and consequently we didn't see him much. I know hat he was making $14.00 or $15.00 a week, but the concept of poverty never came across my mind because there was always some food in the house during those years. He really tried hard. Sometimes he would come home and bring food which wasn't sufficient for us because we were always hungry and he was conscious of his. Sometimes whatever he gave us was not the kind of food we were supposed to eat at that time, but it was food! What-so-ever he could get, was food, and he would give it to us, no matter what the time of day. Between what my father could scrape up and the neighbors, who sometimes fed us, we were not fully conscious of what was really happening until years later.

Then they decided to close the brick yard temporarily, and my father continued to look for work and only picked up a day's work here and there. It finally got to the point where he couldn't pay the rent on the Molten Street house, so we moved to the back of a house which belonged to a person who led the life of a peddler. His name wa s Bubba Belt and he treated us real mean. We knew he always came home at a certain hour drunk, so one night we put a whole lot of chairs and things behind the door, and he fell and broke his arm; but to his credit, he never told on us.

MY FATHER MARRIES AGAIN

The first Molten Street years ended with the death of my mother and the return of the children to Alabama to await my father's selection of a second wife. After we returned to Columbus and my father had married again we briefly lived in another section of Molten Street, which I called the second Molten Street years. They were followed by the Marshallville period.

A year passed between my mother's death, and my father's second marriage. It was during these months that we lived in Alabama with grandmothers and grand aunts, Aunt Liza Miller, my father's father, my Great Grandmother Ma Mary, and a whole host of relatives. There in Union Springs, Alabama where we came from originally, we worked on the farm and did chores and different things and tried to adjust the best we could.

My father didn't have to look for a second wife as I later learned from a relative. He was going with this woman before he married my mother. My mother was his first choice and after she died, he just married the second choice. She was still single so he didn't have to look as long as we thought he did.

When she first saw all of us, she laughed, and I knew then that I wasn't going to like her from that moment. I wasn't going to like her anyway because she was supposed to replace my mother.

They had three children. The first was a girl named Ruby

_ean. We called her Bit, because she was so small. She now
lives in Atlanta with her children, grandchildren, and great
grandchild. She hasn't been well for the past five years. I
have two half brothers, Hugh Oscar Clarke, and Walter
Clarke, who are both retired and living in Columbus. They
all grew up in Columbus, where they went to school, but
Bit later moved to Atlanta as an adult where she raised her
children.

We noticed that Bit and the children of the second wife
got privileges over the children of the first wife. And
because my father was always boasting of his love for his
first wife, we thought it was a contradiction that he would
let his children be mistreated by his second wife, so we
began to drift apart.

I was the only one of the children who had something to
lock up, which I did, in a trunk that an officer who was
moving to another post had given me. Army officers move
very often. One of them gave me a wardrobe trunk that
he wasn't going to take with him. I locked my only
possessions up in this trunk. This made my stepmother
mad; so, she threw it into the yard, drawer by drawer
scattering my personal belongings and little knick knacks
that boys accumulate. She resented the trunk. This helped
me to make my decision to move out. Finally, because I
couldn't get along with my stepmother, I became even
more determined to move. I especially wanted to move

because there was no harmony between my stepmother and the children of the first wife. After I moved, my younger sister, Mary, decided to stay. She eventually moved at fifteen because our step mother treated her so mean, barely giving her clothes to wear or enough food to eat. Mary worked after school and was partially maintaining herself, so she asked Ollie Mae Davis, who was the mother of our sister's girlfriend to take her in. She did, and Mary lived there for a year before she moved to another location. My other sister Flossie was there intermittently. She worked for different white people in different parts of town, and sometimes traveled with them, taking care of their babies. My youngest brother Nathaniel continued to live with our cousin, Betty, until she died. After her death, he returned to live with the rest of the family until his subsequent move to New York. He died here in 1955.

SCHOOL DAYS

I really didn't excel in school because I was kept out of school to work. I was a caddy at the golf course before and after school and on weekends, where I earned a little bit of money which I contributed to my father's household.

I caddied at Fort Benning, Georgia and worked for Dwight Eisenhower and Omar Bradley. They were both majors then, long before they became generals. I especially liked Major Bradley because he tipped more, was a better human being, and without question, was kind to the caddies who carried his bags. I stopped caddying to work for officers in town mowing lawns, and polishing boots. I had these little jobs running errands and doing odd jobs, keeping body and soul together; and was always partly self-sustaining.

One day in class, the teacher asked us to do a composition and I always did my compositions when I had the time. This day I got to school late, and she called on me. I picked up a blank piece of paper and mentally composed a composition. It was the first creative inventive test of my imagination. Then she asked me to pass it in. I had nothing on the paper. Her reaction was that I would, one day, be a writer due to my creative inventiveness. Her name was Miss Harris, and it was the Third Grade in the Fifth Avenue School. She was rather understanding about it, and said next time to start early, and wasn't even bitter or harsh.

15

John Henrik Clarke: The Early Years

I never had a sense of confidence in myself until teacher came to me and told me "as good as you are, you are not doing your best, never give less than your best self." That was Miss Everlina Taylor who taught Fifth Grade. I envisioned Miss Taylor being my Fifth Grade teacher all of my life, because the color system of the school was broken down with Miss Taylor and Miss Den teaching the dark skinned students for that grade. You might say that I had special relationships with my teachers Mrs. Luke who later became Mrs. Wyndanch, was my fourth grade teacher and she and I remained friends up until her death somewhere in the late 1980's. I always went by to see her whenever I went home to Columbus.

I left the Fifth Avenue School, after finishing Sixth Grade there, to go to Spencer High School where the Seventh Grade was. The Seventh Grade was located in the high school due to the overcrowding in the Fifth Avenue School and this was how I ended up in the high school building.

I was late getting to the Seventh Grade which had nothing to do with being smart or being left back, and I understood about not being able to go to school regularly because some children didn't go at all. I had this feeling of wonderment, and also a touch of fear and strangeness of being judged due to improper dress. Since I couldn't impress anyone that way, I had to get my lessons and impress them in that manner. I was able to go to school ıore consistently, after I moved out of my father's house nd went to live with Miss Rosa Lee Brown.

Before I left Columbus, I went to a County School ecause I was alert and could read well. The County School vas the Miller Hills School and was located outside of the ity limits. From there I went to the City School. Only one hild could go from a family that lived outside of the city imits. The children who went to City School wore better :lothes, and had to pay a book fee of $3.75 which came ɔut of their parent's earnings of $12.00 to $15.00 a week. This was big money then. The fact that I was chosen was never quite forgiven by my siblings.

I MOVE INTO MADAM ROSA LEE'S HOUSE

I had to move because there seemed to be a personality thing between my stepmother and my father's children from his first marriage. She didn't like us and had a habit of saying "I married your father, but I'm not your mother."

In looking for a place to stay, I remembered this short stout lady in the community who occasionally wore a wig. Her name was Ms. Rosa Lee Brown. I found her and asked her for a place to stay. She said that she'd put me up. I was fourteen when I left home and was actively supporting myself. I was to replace her natural son who had gone off, I think, to Chicago and never wrote. So I became the substitute for her son and lived in her house for four years. I remember that was the first time I became mindful of wigs. What also stands out in my mind was that when she lost her temper, she would say there was nothing short about her but her hair.

She ran a boarding house on Sixth Avenue and Eighth Street, about where the soldiers got off the bus and looked for the ladies of the evening. Later on during the depression, her boarding house became another kind of house. I have fond memories of the four years with her. I was treated very nicely, even by the other ladies in spite of their profession. When I went to Sunday School, they would all give me money to put in the collection plate. They would even buy books for me, and would give me money to go to the movies. I was family.

Once I had to participate in a school program by making a presentation in assembly. All of the program participants were asked to bring their families. I was estranged from my family. My father couldn't take off and my stepmother wouldn't have taken the time off anyway. So I asked all of the ladies from the house to come. Four of them came, and stood up as my family. Everybody knew their profession, respected them for coming, and respected me for asking them to attend. I could never in life be ashamed of them as they were all I had to show.

There was a rival house next to the one in which I was living, ran by a Madam referred to as Sally Chicken Foot. Competition existed between the two houses, but it wasn't bitter or anything like that. The competition that existed was that the clients were soldiers, all from the same base, but were from different barracks. Sometimes both houses entertained clients from other walks of life. I could never forget Sally Chicken Foot because she had the greatest respect for me because I could read and write. When she'd pay her insurance bills, she'd call me to read the receipts to make sure they were done right. When she learned I had no money to go to New York and that I was going hobo, and saw me passing on the way to the railroad yard, she said something that would stimulate me to this day, in spite of the way she said it. She said, "There goes a Nigger who someday will be something that the rest of us Niggers will someday feel proud of." It was the greatest contribution to my spirit.

NEW YORK IN THE EARLY 1930'S

When my friend, James Holmes, and I decided to leave Georgia for the North, we took the first freight car that had fruits, vegetables and hobos on one end, and an empty ice box section that had a cover over it at the other end, which we left ajar. The year was 1933.

Now, if you're riding in something like that, and the cover slips close, you can suffocate from the lack of air, and you can do this before you know what's happening. Experienced hobos, generally put something around the edge so that there would be some air to prevent this from happening; but unfortunately, this did not always work.

We changed trains in Chicago for the next available freight that would take us closest to New York. It was our good fortune that this train went to New Jersey.

Pulling into New Jersey, with the yard people assuming that there was always someone inside of the freight cars, made them knock along the cars with sticks. Of course we came out, to find them not harsh, bitter or anything. They just showed us out of the yard, and chased us away from the trains, and from there we walked to the ferry which would take us to New York. The ferries then were a nickel a ride from New Jersey to New York. We caught one and asked some people how to get to Harlem, which cost us another nickel. That was for carfare, which added up to twenty cents of our small fortune, now gone. We didn't have more than fifty cents between us, but we still took the subway and went to Harlem, and arrived at the Harlem Y.

I had recommendations from all of the good work I had done at the YMCA in my hometown, and the good work had done in school. I was a bright young lad, but that didn't impress the snooty middle class executives at the Harlem Y. So they sent us to the municipal lodging house This was a flop house, not far from where Bellevue Hospital in now located. That's where they sent us and we stayed there the night.

In order to stay there, we went through the ordeal of the interview, showered under supervision, and had a medical examination to see if we had gonorrhea or syphilis. All of this was before we got fully inside the building. It was after we were admitted that we were then directed to one of these bunk bed things for the night.

In the morning we decided this wasn't the place for us, so we wandered around the Lower East Side. Someone told us of a newsboy's home where newsboys could stay, but we didn't know enough about New York to even pretend that we were New York newsboys. However, we went there anyway. They gave us all kinds of advice but they didn't give us any place to stay. Then they sent us to a welfare type place for men where you sawed wood for

John Henrik Clarke: The Early Years

fifty cents. So we both got fifty cents and both bought a loaf of bread and a can of sardines, then made a single loaf sandwich. We split the whole loaf in half, opened it up, scatered the sardines throughout and poured the juice around. That was our meal for the rest of the day.

We maneuvered quite well with the fifty cents and continued to wander around, where we occasionally got a dollar for helping somebody load a truck. We made a dollar or fifty cents and just survived, by helping to load trucks at the Fulton Fish Market.

We hung around the Lower East Side for three days where there was a place called the Bum's Market. That was interesting. It was under the wing of the Brooklyn Bridge where people traded everything: old shoes, underwear, shirts, old furniture and things they had stolen that everybody knew was stolen.

By the middle of our first week, when we were not too far from a building called the Journal American (there used to be a Hearst newspaper called the Journal American for which this building was named). One of the workers, who was well dressed, came up to us and introduced himself. We told him we were looking for a place. He took us to a restaurant and bought us a meal and told us he'd take us to find some place to stay. Years later, we wondered whether he was a homosexual. We didn't suspect that then, and as it turned out he wasn't.

John Henrik Clarke: The Early Years

That was fortunate for us, because if he was, we wouldn' have known how to handle the situation anyway. He was a Russian who called himself George Victor.

He was the person who really gave us a home, shelter and food for a little while, and immediately began to introduce us to the concept of communism. He would make statements like, "This lousy capitalistic system is the cause of your condition." And so we listened during the night to his tirades against capitalism, which involved me listening primarily and was my introduction to reading matter I had never known before.

I kept active in the Young Communist League on the Lower East Side, and there on the Lower East Side, I met a young Black man, then active in the Brooklyn Communist Party. He was from the South and was married to a young white girl named Fern. The rumor was that they were both from a Southern City, and when it was discovered that they were going together, they had to escape. They had one baby, a girl, who was in the cradle at the time. I remember the young man once being evicted for not paying rent. His name was Henry Winston. He is dead now. He was one of the communists tried at Foley Square, was beaten in jail, and subsequently went blind. Through the years prior to his death, we remained pretty good friends. He was an excellent theoretician who wrote the book *Strategy for a Black Agenda*.

John Henrik Clarke: The Early Years

While I was a valuable member of the Young Communist League and even a valuable young fellow traveler, I always had a difference of opinion of party cultism. I resented the fact that Karl Marx had all the answers, and that nothing else was to be considered. I always had conflict with that.

The main thing here, is that, I began to meet some of the early revolutionary workers during that period and began to read their literature, among which was the literature of James Allen's reconstruction communist view of the aftermath of the Civil War. I began to reconsider W.E.B. DuBois' work and saw no conflict between Nationalism, Pan Africanism and Communism. All this was at eighteen!

During this era, I began an examination of the position of the world in relationship to what it could do for my own people. A small antagonism between the left and myself, began to emerge based on the fact that I saw no contradiction on placing the love of my people first. I basically believed that, ultimately, a sharing society would have to come into being to have any society at all, because capitalism is without humanity, without heart, and without concern for people. People who are willing to work should have a decent way of life for having done so. I thought that then, and still do. My beliefs came out of my experience as a sharecropper in Alabama and Georgia. I didn't need to read Karl Marx to think this; it just made sense.

These were the formative years of my career. It was the great turning point in my life when my awareness of Garveyism was heightened. I became a part of the Garvey movement that was revived in Harlem. I visited the Garvey clubs and attended most of the free lectures pertaining to culture, politics and history that placed emphasis on African people.

My maturing and the shaping of my manhood would come in the years of the Italian - Ethiopian War. At the time, I was a member of a History Club that changed its name to the Edward Wilmot Blyden Society after the great Caribbean scholar Edward Wilmot Blyden. Kwame Nkrumah, who would become the first President of Ghana, visited the club; also, the great pacifist, John Hayes Holmes, visited the club once in a while and spoke to us. John Jackson, who now lives in Chicago, was active in the club; and, with Dr. Willis N. Huggins, wrote a book called *A Guide to the Study of African History*. Later they would write the *Introduction to African Civilization*. John had done some monumental pamphlets. He had taken the origins of the Christ myth, and the African origin of the Legend of the Garden of Eden and presented these works in the Chapel of the Harlem Y which seated about sixty people. As part of these presentations at the Y, I delivered a lecture called "An Inquiry into the Ethnic Identity of Jesus Christ," out of which would come the short story *The Boy Who Painted Christ Black.*

I witnessed the first Harlem Riot around 1935. I would embrace all this and afterwards, I would leave those years with a kind of understanding that would be with me for the rest of my life, on how the world was run, for whom it was run, and how it got that way in the first place.

I was enlightened by Dr. Huggins, the great master teacher, who talked not just history, but the political meaning of history. Arthur Schomburg, who presided over the special book collection at the public library on 135th Street, taught me comparative study of history, which was an invaluable lesson. I also met J. A. Rogers, Charles C. Seifort and many other writers and teachers who had devoted most of their lives to the study and teaching of African history. Later from Leo Hansberry, I would learn of the philosophical meaning of history.

I followed these men with great devotion, and read most of the books they recommended. See, when I look back on it, I now realize that I was learning from these masters, outside of college, certain things no college would ever have given me, all of which I have since tried to give my students. I am talking about not just the recitation of facts, but what it all means in relation to the world.

ARTHUR SCHOMBURG

Arthur Schomburg was never too busy to talk to me. He was even approachable to my greatest surprise. On meeting him for the first time, I approached him requesting to know the whole history of my people henceforth, within the hour. He proceeded to tell me that I should, first, really study European history in relation to the history of African people and their culture; and said that I would never fully understand the history of our people, until I had studied world history.

When he saw me reading a certain book, and knew there was something better on the subject, he would come over and point me in the right direction. During the four years I knew him, from 1934 to 1938, he showed me exactly how our history was stolen; shared Paul Lawrence Dunbar's letters to the *Saturday Evening Post* with me, Charles Chestnut's letters to his wife when he was away from home, and other documents of great significance. A lot of people visited the library who just simply took up space and time, but he recognized that I was searching for something special. He saw in me a kind of potential and was always patient. Sometimes, I would confront him on his lunch hour, while he worked at the front desk.

When the little groups, to which I belonged realized that I knew him, they always asked me to get him for programs because nobody had money to pay for speakers in those days. I never wrote him a note. I would just go over and ask him to speak to the group. He would accept, and was always gracious and impeccably dressed, usually in the same dark brown suit.

I did not know what a profound influence Arthur Schomburg had on my life, until I began to look back at how I met him literally, I mean historically, by reading his essay in the book *The New Negro*. The essay was called, "The Negro Digs Up His Past." This was really the first major essay that I had read showing that African people had a past and a history longer than Europe. I later wrote a poem about it, which merely said that we were older than our oppressors and that we would outlive these oppressors.

In the years of talking to Schomburg and meeting him at the subway, walking him to the door of the library, together with reading about the great works of Hansberry, these instances are what I call the meaningful turning points in my life. All this and still in my twenties!

It's sad to repeat what really killed him. He had an abscessed tooth, and the doctor told him that he needed dental surgery which cost $10.00. An extraction cost $2.00. He debated on whether or not to spend the $10.00, and while he labored over the decision, the poison from the tooth traveled into his system and killed him. This is the information of his death that was reported to me. I discovered Schomburg's death while reading the New York Times. I was a dishwasher and an assistant cook in a luncheonette, off Williams Street, called Nan McKenzie's, run by a Scotch lady and an Englishman. When I was apparently slow in washing the dishes and preparing the vegetables for the cook, and was not aware that there were tears in my eyes, they asked me what was wrong. They weren't unkind or anything, they just wanted to know what was wrong with me, and were concerned, humanly concerned. I was a good worker, and now I was slowing down and moping. I told them that a dear friend, Arthur Schomburg, had passed; and, they tried to understand.

That evening after I finished work, going home seemed to have taken longer than ever before, and I didn't know what I was going home to do except to brood over the loss. Everything seemed slower, and there didn't seem to be anything that I could do about it. My walking seemed slower and every time I tried to walk around people, they seemed to consistently get in my way. Finally, I got into the subway and the subway seemed to move slower than usual. I got out of the subway and was moving step by step toward that little furnished room where I lived at 128th Street off Lenox Avenue, and my steps that seemed to move me forward didn't seem to move me closer to the room. When I finally got in the room and began a quiet, nward crying that went on for quite sometime, I understood the nature of the loss and what was left.

What was left, were my friends in the group called the National League of Negro Youth, the great master teacher, Willis N. Huggins of the Harlem History Club who taught me the political meaning of history; his protege, John G. Jackson, who had emphasized the role of religion and the interplay of history as a power in human existence; my associates on the fringe of the Garvey Movement, and the activity that I engaged in during and after the Italian - Ethiopian War.

What I want to say is that intellectually, I was maturing and growing up. I was beginning to understand the nature of the teaching of Arthur Schomburg, to understand the history of African people and its relationship to the history of the world, and I knew then that I had to build on the foundation that Arthur Schomburg had shown me how to lay. While, of course, his physical body was gone, the spirit of the man was very firm inside of me and that spirit would be part of my total education that in that university without walls that was the Harlem community, he had been one of my finest teachers. I had lost one great teacher, but still had great teachers left; they too would point me into other directions and continue to show me a meaning of history over and above what any university could have given me.

ARMY LIFE

Before I went into the army, I read enough books and attended enough lectures to give myself the equivalent of a college education.

Prior to leaving for basic training, I received word that my father had died. Although he had been relatively well, his death did not come as a complete surprise. He couldn't afford a mere $5.00 waist belt that he needed for the lifting and the hard work he did. As a result, he strained himself and developed a hernia. He died at a comparatively young age from these complications and a stroke. Five dollars could have saved him.

I entered the army on September 9, 1941 at Camp Upton on Long Island. I didn't stay there very long before I was sent to Davis Field in Tucson, Arizona, where my company did practically nothing but porter work and cleaning up bushes. It was discovered after three months that the Army had lost us on paper and we should not have been sent to that post in the first place.

Next they sent us to San Antonio, Texas for our regular assignment which was going to be a Truck Company, eventually, because most of the men had been trained as truck drivers. While I had basic training as a truck driver, at this point I really had not ever even driven a car, although

I finished with a high grade in mechanics. I knew the theory well enough to pass on the exam, but didn't have the practice to time a motor, which was very basic. I think I could change a tire and shift gears. However, I had not driven a car so much as ten blocks, yet I had the theory down.

Our arrival in San Antonio might have been traumatic, but I just don't think that we had time enough to suffer shock because it was so contradictory, dealing with a form of schizophrenia and the white Southerner, especially white Southern officers. A captain came out massaging one hand against the other with great joy and said boldly, happily, "Proud to see you Niggers, nicest bunch of Niggers I've seen in a long time. As you can see most of the soldiers on this base are living in tents. I expected you boys and to show you how much I think of you, I saved the barracks for you, with running water and everything." Then he reminded us that there were only one hundred fifty-five of us and probably ten thousand of the others. So he said, "You boys are going to behave yourselves aren't you?" Well, we got the point.

That was Captain Carmichael, and the men were in shock. They shook their heads and said what they were going to do to him and called him a SOB under their breath. Yet, in the next three years, the best favors we were going to have and the best protection we were going to get would come from Captain Carmichael. He became Provost Marshall, the equivalent to the head of the Military Police. He also became a Colonel in that short time.

He would give me a pass so that I could go into town and sign my men out of jail, for any minor offense. I mean just sign my name and take them out of jail, back to the company and punish them. When I went into town, I would pass by the jails to see who I could sign out. Sometimes it would be 11 o'clock at night when I arrived and the men would say, "Where the hell were you?" They were jailed for minor things like fighting in the streets and so on, and had no business being there at all.

The Commander of the Company was Captain Forrester who was a Midwesterner and a perfectionist. He taught "enlisted men administration (which was supply administration)," and he taught me well. He didn't have much time to teach me, because he was really part of the administration on the post and he was a Commander as additional duty. So he could only come there once or twice a day and look at things and sign the morning report. So, we were almost self sustained by a Sergeant. I was promoted from buck private to a three stripe sergeant, and I was head of the supply room. I moved up in rank because I was in a company that had all open rank, which had mobility. If I was in a company that had a whole lot of ergeants already, there would be no mobility. So I began to move up, and it was decided that all Supply Sergeants would be automatically promoted to Staff Sergeant. So I became a Staff Sergeant. Then another order came down that Supply Sergeants would be promoted to Tech Sergeants, and that they would be automatically Mess Sergeants and Acting First Sergeants. So, I became a Tech Sergeant and hadn't been in the army for two full years. That was a good promotion. I knew my business. I knew supplies. I ran a good mess hall, and began to run it the same way I ran a restaurant on 126th Street and Lenox Avenue. I served no meal that I wasn't willing to eat myself. As simple as that.

A Black Puerto Rican, named Lorenzo, who got angry for being on K.P. put some soap in the cabbage; so from then on, as I wanted to see no more disgruntled people on K.P., I decided that every time someone served on K.P., I would give them long duty, meaning all of the next day off. The men wanted that because they could go into town and shack up for a long time, as it was a soldier town and the girls were used to seeing the soldiers. So the men were glad to do K.P. to get that long duty. Now I had people doing K.P. who wanted to do it. Therefore, they weren't going to spoil the food. We had the last of those great cooks from Tuskegee. It's true that we got them quite by accident, but we got them anyway, and I was determined to make good use of them.

I became a wizard in the army. I learned military administration, and I learned regulation. I did favors for men. I got people out of the army who otherwise would never have gotten out far ahead of time, because I knew not only the manipulation of regulation; that is, not by faking the law, but by using the law strategically. I studied it for the little stipulations and regulations, saying that a soldier could be dismissed for lack of the required degree of adaptability. This only meant that he wasn't adaptable to military service, which had to be documented. Most administrative sergeants were too damn lazy to document it because when those papers went to a medical board, they had to be air tight and it takes a few days and nights to write up that rationale which is almost like writing a thesis. It was the soldier's medical history, his military history, and his petition for discharge on an honorable basis. He could get a dishonorable discharge because the army would be glad to give a dishonorable discharge, discharging them from all responsibility with the soldier - you know - no pension, and no rights. They just got rid of you and swept you out.

I wrote up the petitions, then got the company's approval for the petition. For one person, named Paxton, who was just a chronic alcoholic, I proved that his lcoholism was aggravated by military service. In civilian life, this man became an executive, and a good one. He became head of North Carolina Insurance Mutual for the whole state of Virginia. He was a little fellow who was brilliant as a whip, who just wouldn't leave that bottle alone.

I enjoyed the challenge of the job in the army. I couldn't drill, and couldn't shoot. In administration, I found something I could do so well, that they would leave me alone to do it. You would have thought that I was a great administrator. I received the best inspections in the whole area, and was a wizard with the adding machine, and can barely multiply nine times nine now.

I did a number of things. When I first looked over the mess hall menu and saw asparagus on it, knowing that my men didn't eat asparagus, I went to one of the white companies and traded my asparagus off for something else.

The army's rules weren't that difficult, once you picked up a book and studied it. But the rules running a mess hall made no kind of sense at all, especially the storage of dry beans. The bins had to be several inches apart and had to have some ventilation at the top. I had it designed because I knew a few carpenters; so I did that just the way they said it should be done, because I knew when I got inspected, that's what they would be looking for.

There wasn't noticeably more drinking in the army than in civilian life. A few men, just like in civilian life, made a mission out of it. They had to have that little nip, and some didn't straighten out until they got it. Some even bootlegged it from the mess hall, and I knew it. You can't stop every little crime because the men had to have some fun. Basically, they got what they wanted, and I got what I wanted, plus we had enough to eat. And we even had our own butcher in the company, who did a good job once he was sober.

GRACE

Now, I'm coming to New York on my first furlough by way of St. Louis (St. Louis was the terminal point); and I see this lady on the train with this little boy, and I help her by taking the boy to the bathroom. She's good looking and everybody's doing anything for her trying to make a pass at her. I'm the only one who's not making a pass at her, or indicating it in any way. I was just taking care of the little boy, speaking to her normally and asked the boy to come sit with me for a little while. Then he went over to sit near her and she came over to sit near me. Her name was Grace.

And she begins to tell me the story about how her husband had gotten killed in a squabble with some soldiers and that there were two, maybe three sets of fingerprints on the gun and there were some questions as to who fired it. And she said that it wasn't such a good marriage because his family considered her an outsider. And there was a girl who he grew up with that both families had chosen and agreed he would marry, and this girl was still waiting for him to return and marry her. He had gone away to college and married Grace instead, who wasn't welcome in the town or in the family. That made things kind of difficult for her, but she did have his child and except for that, she would have turned around and gone back to Ohio. She said that she didn't think tha justice was done for her husband - that some smart aleck sergeant manipulated the papers to make it appear tha there was some doubt as to the soldiers' fingerprints being on the gun; instead of punishing the soldiers, he just shipped them out of the company. Grace said, "Well he was my husband, so something ought to be done about it." See, she did feel that something needed to be done because he was her husband; and as his wife she wanted to see that justice was done but she didn't know where to turn. See, her husband, was a local policeman, and there weren't that many Black policeman in town, maybe six or seven.

I knew she was talking about me. I was the little military administrative wizard who juggled the papers. See, you can make out military charges in such a way that you can convict a man before he came to court or free him. When we got to St. Louis, I took her to dinner in the station. She had a two-hour wait, and my wait was for one hour. I explained to her that when you're in the army, there are two worlds; the civilian world, as opposed to the military world. You fight to save everybody in your world, and you give the benefit of the doubt to your world. I gave the soldier the benefit of the doubt. Her husband was a name on a piece of paper. I never saw his face. I knew the circumstances, but in the army we considered all police the enemy, Black, white, or otherwise. And so I was protecting them from the mythological enemy. I told her that I was the sergeant who manipulated the papers, and she understood.

As her train pulled into the station, she gave me her phone number and said to call her when I got back, and I gave her my phone number at the post and told her about when I would be back, as I had a two week furlough. So when I got back, about a week passed and I had not called her. She called me and said, "I thought you were going to call me and come by." I was just busy with all the accumulated things and refilling of supplies as I was running the mess hall, the orderly room and office all at the same time. But, after her call, I went by the next day. It was Thursday, and it was her day off. She had told me when we were in St. Louis that Thursdays were her days off. She worked at the post in one of the army hangers, putting things together for the Department of Defense. We worked right on the same post, where I was stationed.

When I went to see her, we didn't do very much or even talk about very much. I think we played a hand of cards and talked about high school backgrounds, and I told her about my background before I went into the army. I was wearing these army shoes and felt I had to hide them, and she said that she knew soldiers had to wear army shoes and couldn't dress up finely. Then she laughed and said, "I would really like to see you in civilian clothes." I said that would bring some clothes to her place one of these day and close the door, dress up and just walk around for her and she laughed. After that, during her lunch hour in the evening, like six or seven, I used to walk up to the hange where she was working, same post now, just a differen section. Sometimes, I would have lunch ready for he when she got there, and everybody thought that she wa exceptional and that I must have been real exceptiona too. Sometimes, when I'd go to the mess hall and ask the Mess Sergeant to fix something real nice for her like a sandwich or something and a drink, he did. We would take it into the little dinky room they had for colored, and we would sit there on the bench and eat. When she needed sugar, I would give her fifty pounds of G.I. sugar and butter, whatever she needed. If I would count up all the things I did for her with military funds, I would still be in jail today serving time.

And there was a light skin, halfway good looking fella pursuing her, so the idea now among everybody was who was going to get her - the yellow one or the Black one. And so, one evening when she was telling me about the gossip, she said, "They wanted to know whether you've kissed me yet?" So the next time when I was at her house, I told her that whatever we did was our business, and that, after I left that evening, she wouldn't have to wonder

John Henrik Clarke: The Early Years

anymore whether or not I'd kissed her.

I introduced her to the men and told them that this was my special lady, and I wanted it clearly understood that whenever they saw her in town or any place, she was to be given the same treatment as though she was my legal wife. She liked that. Whenever she visited the post, I would have the men take her home in a military car, and I instructed them to go by the back road, and deposit her at home.

The most important thing that I remember about her is that we could achieve the maximum result, with the minimum amount of physical contact and be thoroughly satisfied with each other. And because we were so satisfied in so many other ways, we just didn't need to be athletes in that way at every meeting.

I remember, one day, when I went to her house and didn't have to go back to the post the next day, because it was Sunday, that we talked late. Her child was away with her sister and we had the house all to ourselves. Naturally, I would take off my military attire and just walk around in my shirt sleeves and socks while we talked, joked and touched each other. We didn't do anything too alluring or special, but she looked at the clock later that night and said, "It's three o'clock in the morning; we should go to bed." And she started laughing and said, "All this time and we haven't made love." "Come to think of it, that's what we've been having all evening." See, she understood the higher meaning of a relationship -- that the higher meaning of a relationship is not necessarily the physical act, but to make people so completely pleased and at ease, one to the other; that the joy of being with each other is tantamount to it and more than a substitute. Very few relationships reach that point and that tone where they can achieve that. I know one thing, I never achieved it again with another person. I guess very few of us find the person who is absolutely right for us or almost so, and very few of us make that connection and keep that connection. I guess I am no different from anyone else in that regard. And so it was from this point that we began a relationship which is in my mind still, the most beautiful relationship I have ever had with a woman.

Her brother was the first Black to be the head of a music department in a white school. He was head of the Music Department at Antioch and had a position with the National Endowment for the Arts, until he retired. He had an apartment in Washington, and when he wasn't using it, he would offer me the key on my visits to Washington. I never took him up on it.

By the time I was getting out of the army, although my relationship with Grace had not cooled, she had grown impatient with my inability to straighten out my life so that I could give her some explicit answer as to what the

wo of us were going to do. She began to see someone
emporarily and would call me once in awhile, and we
would go horseback riding.

I remember, while horseback riding in a white area, she
said, "This is where white people come to play." And,
when we got back to the Black area and passed a Black
church, I said, "This is where Black people go to pray," and
pointed out that there was a world of difference between
the players and the prayers and that the prayers had no
power.

There were a whole lot of other men bidding for her
favor, and she couldn't quite make up her mind. She later
married a sergeant in my company. He had been
previously married to a lawyer's daughter. He played
around, and finally got caught. What I didn't like about
him was that he was always boasting about what he
would or wouldn't do, and "that he didn't hang out with
nothing that wasn't pretty." His stand was clear. As far as I
was concerned, while he was basically a good human
being, I'm of the opinion that he lacked principles. The
reason why I didn't marry Grace is because I was involved
in a relationship with a girl here in New York that I had
known as a teenager, who had a child by me. I was taking
care of her and the child as best I could, and wanted to
straighten that matter out so Grace and I could get
together. It was never successfully straightened out, and I

eventually married the child's mother. Had I been a irresponsible human being, and not taken care of m responsibility to my daughter's mother, I might hav pursued another course in my life.

After I got out of the army and returned to New Yor and started to adjust myself, taking care of my child by m first wife, Grace came to New York to see me.

There was something in my communication with he that I liked and never found again, and she is the one woman I will regret, to my dying day, that I did not marry

CAREER BEGINNINGS AFTER THE ARMY

I left the service in late 1945, about November, and returned to New York. I didn't work on a regular basis for the next six months. I kept looking and trying to get my bearings as I still had to find money to support my child. It was difficult, and all these things were a terrible drain on my time and energy.

I returned with the hope of going to school and getting my writing career started. It was difficult because, by being a correspondent clerk in the army, I had learned almost a different style of writing; and once I was out of the army, I had to learn how to adjust myself to a whole new different kind of writing, and to write fluid sentences again that had decorative words other than the abruptness of the army like "approved," "disapproved," "referred as a matter pertaining to your command," "say nothing of excess." The army did not believe in dealing with an excess in words. They just came straight to the point.

I was offered a job at the Veterans Administration that had almost guaranteed security. But I turned it down, wanting to write, go to school and find myself. The child's mother was rather abrasive about me turning it down. She thought I was jeopardizing their welfare because that would have been an assured income. Because at that time, with my military recommendations and with my skills, would have been a Grade XII Civil Service Worker in five years. I didn't accept the position, and that started a dissension between me and my child's mother that never ended.

I then tried to go back to some of the old things that didn't work, and began to do a little newspaper work that didn't pay very much, and took whatever job was available to me.

I took a clerk's position with the Board of Education in Long Island where they made up lunches and distributed them to the different schools. I brought my military efficiency to the job, because I didn't know how to string the work out into a full day. You got all school holidays off, went in about five in the morning and got out a little after twelve. It was nice.

I left there after awhile and was doing other jobs. Maybe it would have been in my best interest to stay there. However, I tried to get into the Post Office as a temporary Christmas employee with the hope that with some of the veterans who were taken on as Christmas employees, I would become one of the regulars. I didn't get that, and things weren't working too well for me until I eventually took a job, as a manager of a night snack bar at LaGuardia Airport. I supposedly made a pretty decent salary there, which wasn't much, but with the tips, I some-

mes made $60, $70, or $80 a week. It allowed me to take
are of my family rather nicely while living in a big
urnished room off 136th Street and Eighth Avenue,
where I was getting my writing career gradually
nderway, still not making enough money. I lived in that
oom almost seventeen years in between marriages. I
ventually married the mother of my daughter, right
here, and my brother Nathaniel - who was always very
upportive of me, who had a great deal of respect for me -
vas my best man.

Now, between the little bit of money I was making and
along with the G.I. Bill, I began to write and go to New
York University. Along with going to New York University
between 1949 and 1950, I started to edit the Harlem
Quarterly, and became active in the Harlem Writer's Guild
with John Killens and others. This group lasted longer
than any other Black Writer's group in the country, and is
still intact.

We met at John Killens' house, where a bit of John's
early writings were done, and it's there where I first met
Lorraine Hansberry, who was beginning to get her writing
career together.

Harold Cruz was also a member of the group. He would
later write about different crises and the Negro
intellectual. He was a sore head who attempted to attack
all the members of his old gang who got out of the mire

before he did. His attack on Richard Moore, and his attack on Lorraine Hansberry was all in error. As I said before, he was just a sore head, who got so many facts wrong.

When I began to teach, I began to teach on the community level, and started my career as a community activist at that point. I became a part-time teacher, and worked at the New School for Social Research and assisted in setting up the Africana Studies Center, the Center for African Studies, along with Stanford Griffith. It was at this time, around 1956 or 1957 that I also helped to bring Leo Hansberry to the New School, and tried to start saving for my eventual trip to Africa.

FROM AFRICA TO EUROPE

My first trip to Africa was for three months in 1958. I went mainly to Ghana; and while in Ghana, I went to Nigeria and Togo. I went in the Summer and returned in the Fall. I had wanted to go to Africa all of my life, and prepared for it mentally for most of my life, but still had to go on borrowed funds. Arriving in Ghana, felt like I had returned home.

I had written a short story, *The Boy Who Painted Christ Black,* that was reprinted in *Drum Magazine* in South Africa and circulated in Ghana. As a result, people began to write me short letters, and I received a letter from a young man in Ghana. I wrote him back and told him that I planned to be in Ghana the next year and that I was going to stay in a hotel for one week, and wanted to stay in a home with African people for the rest of my stay in Ghana. Upon my arrival in Ghana, my pen pal James Kotey met me at the airport, and took me straight to his home where I stayed. We are still friends, and I still hear from him. He is a chief section meter reader for the Ghanaian Electrical Department, and should be retiring this year.

While I was in Ghana, I lived in a family compound with the Ga people. The Ga people are different than other Akan people. Most of Ghana consists of Akan people, together with the major ethnic families in Ghana.

Nkrumah was from the Twi branch of the Akan. H
discovered me after I had been in Ghana for awhile and
gave me a job on his newspaper *The Evening News*
Working for the newspaper allowed me to study the
opposition in Ghana and the party in power, and I could
see right there where Ghana was going wrong, ever
where Nkrumah was going wrong by trying to develop ar
African Socialism without paying much attention to
African traditionalism.

I got to learn Nkrumah's supporters and the opposition.
also learned about Nkrumah's teacher, Joseph B
Danquah; and of his anger because Nkrumah did not use
African traditionalism, especially in developing his concept
of socialism.

Danquah knew, as Nkrumah did not live to know, that
most European based ideas of socialism would not work in
an African setting, unless you infused them with those
African concepts of socialism that had no name. You see,
the Africans became socialists without using the word
"socialists," they became Christians without using the
word "Christians," and they were democratic without
using the word "democracy." In Africa, you never say, "I
am my brother's keeper." You just keep him.

Ghana was the ideal place to get Africa's Independence
freedom explosion underway. You basically had a
homogeneous population in Ghana. While they had

differences of opinion and minor wars, they never fought each other to the point of extinction, or used wars to fight into death, or into anything that lasted so long that the bitterness would resound down through the years.

While visiting Africa, I could also see where Nigeria wasn't completely independent, but was on the verge of independence, and I saw certain Nigerians who assisted the British by doing so. I also noticed that Nigeria had a different kind of culture, was culturally diverse, and that these cultures were not trained to work together. The framework was not there. The Hausa-Fulani, who were essentially Muslims, had conflict among themselves and also an additional conflict with the Yoruba and the Igbos.

Some of the best writing I've done is on my travels in Ghana, and I wrote several pieces on travels in Africa. I wrote a long piece on my bus trip from Ghana to Nigeria which I called *Journey from Accra to Lagos*, and was going to put several travel pieces into a book and call it *Africa Without Tears*. When I returned from Africa, I had the first book finished, but no publisher was interested in anything about Africa that wasn't dirty, smutty, or cheap gossip like who the presidents or heads of state were sleeping with, and how many mistresses they had. That kind of thing didn't interest me at all, now or then. I didn't want to write books like that. After Nkrumah's death, they were looking for something to write a spicy book on and discovered that he only had one lone mistress. When I heard this, I just shrugged my shoulder and said, for a president of a country that was kind of skimpy.

On this trip, I stopped in London on my way to Ghana and in Rome and Paris on my way back. When I got to England, I was to briefly meet the large contingent o Caribbean writers. England, London especially, was to the Caribbean writer what Paris once was to other writers, like the Black American writers. Richard Wright was in Paris at the time I was in London, and I met Richard Gibson and Ollie (Oliver) Harrington who did the cartoon Bootsie. George Lamming was kind of my host, and a beautiful host he was. He took me to see Eric Waldron of Panama and Jamaica. Waldron was not in the best of spirits. He was a writer who had participated in the Harlem Renaissance; second of the great voices of the Renaissance, second only to Claude McKay. He had written the famous classic novel *Tropic Death,* about the exploitation of Jamaican workers in the Panama Canal, so he was a person who had established himself well in the Black community and in the Caribbean community where he was well thought of. He kind of thought the world had forgotten him at the time - forgotten all the different things he had done and he was almost in a quiet rage. In fact, he thought that he was a "has been."

He greeted me well, but he had no high opinion of the

new writers coming on the scene, getting all the attention he thought he should have gotten. He liked the fact that I still remembered him with great respect. For all the reviews he did in the old *Crisis Magazine* and the old *Opportunity Magazine* published by the Urban League, you know I respect that. That was the first and last time I was to see him alive.

I never dreamed that one day I would meet his daughter. Her name is Lucille. Her married name is Meir. When I first met her, she was a professor at the University of the West Indies, at the Mona Campus, in Jamaica. She is presently the Permanent Representative from Jamaica to the United Nations, and is a very important person. In fact, she called me recently.

Did I tell you that I stayed in London for about five days, and was to briefly meet the literary crew there? While in London, I would discover what Alex Haley would later announce, that London had more information per square yard that almost any other place in the world. I mean, there are libraries and documentary centers, specialized libraries, and her Majesty's Stationary Office which is equivalent to a government printing office here. Then there was the British Museum, its vast library, plus every museum had its own library in a basement with things that were not even shown, that only specialized people got to see. Then there was the colonial library, and the public record's library. I would get to go into some of these libraries. Others, I didn't get into until many years later.

I went to the British Museums, and visited a lot of England's second hand bookstores, like the ones we have on Fourteenth Street, in New York. I also spent a great deal of time in the second hand bookstores off Piccadilly Square, and I visited Foyles which used to be one of the most famous bookstores in the world, and Blackwells' Bookstore in Oxford, England. Getting to Oxford, which is a suburb of London, is like going from New York to Long Island by taking a short train ride. I have had an account there for thirty years or more. Then there's Dillards near the University of London, where you could go and just go crazy for books you've wanted to read all of your life.

The British are great readers. They use books creatively. They don't read "at" the book; they read the book when we just scan it. You have a strong intellectual class in England that's poor, who can discuss the affairs of the world with you. We don't have that kind of class here. So, I stopped in London on my way to Ghana, in Paris on my way back, and spent almost ten days in Rome.

Coming through Rome returning from Africa, while waiting for the convening of the Second International Congress of African Writers to meet in Rome, I learned through the American Embassy that the meeting was postponed and was going to be held in Paris. So I went to Paris. But I spent almost ten days in Rome where I first visited the Coliseum a lot, the Vatican, a number of times, and other historical sites there. This was my way of studying history on the spot. I remember when I went to the Vatican, that I saw, in the small catacombs, evidence still of Black saints, especially of the Madonnas.

I had time to learn the Roman bus system, which I learned from the clerks at the hotel. It was not complicated at all, and far less complicated than the one in New York City.

Crossing the streets in Rome was like risking your life, because the big wide streets had practically no street lights and every cop you went to was a special kind of cop. Sometimes a traffic cop would say he was a metropolitan cop, or another kind of cop would say he wasn't suppose to handle that, so you never knew what kind of policeman to speak to when you wanted specialized information. They were also well dressed and I think their mission was to get their picture taken with the tourists. Anyway, I enjoyed the week in Rome. I enjoyed the Italians as a people, and got to know them better in Rome than I did in New York. Italian people have a beautiful temperament, which is different from those in New York City and different from the French who can be a little abrasive and abrupt. They always want to know if you are enjoying yourself, truly welcome you, are glad to see you and curious about your being in their city. The normal tourist hustle that you get in Paris and London is not quite as apparent in Rome.

The short subway system in Rome is something in which they took so much pride. They closed it down at 1 a.m., to keep unsavory characters out. Of course, that was in 1958. I don't know what they're doing with it now.

My visit to Rome was very pleasant. I learned that once you get to know Europeans, many of them have a certain levelness in their temperament, and these are people with an infusion of Black blood in them.

So when I finally proceeded to Paris to see who was gathered for the conference, I learned that it was also postponed for another time. Once in Paris, I enjoyed meeting some of the great stalwarts and leading figures in the intellectual community. Mercer Cook was there at the time, John Davis and that group from the American Society of African Culture along with Ted Harris. The American contingent was visible in Paris with men like Richard Allen, the famous poet, and other outstanding writers. Aimé Cesaire was there from Martinique and Cheikh Anta Diop was there studying. I didn't get to know him then, but would get to know him better a little later on, even though I was acquainted with his work at that time.

Another person I did get to meet very briefly was Renée Moran, who had written a book called *Back to Allah* in 1922, and won the French equivalent of the Pulitzer Prize for it. He was the governor of one of the areas in French Equatorial Africa, who moved to Paris and married a French lady, and had edited a magazine called *The Cries of the Negro*.

I was to be introduced to the French speaking community in such a way that the friendships would last until this very day. Even today, I probably have better communication with their community than with almost any other Black American scholar; with maybe, the exception of Richard Long, who speaks French fluently and is a person who reads and communicates well with French speaking Africa. He was at Atlanta University; but, now teaches at Emory University. Overall, the trip was beneficial.

RETURN FROM AFRICA TO MY HOME IN EXILE

Coming home was a big transition after living in Africa, traveling into the hinterlands and getting to know African people.

I resembled so many African people because of my physical flexibility. Therefore, many Africans came up to me and started speaking to me in their language as one of them, and it was then that I realized the friendly contact the African people had with other African people.

One time when I went to Northern Ghana and was up there for a few weeks, I hadn't seen a white man for days and days. I thought about growing up in Georgia, and the fact that almost every white man was a policeman; how every white person caused a little fear when you saw them, man or woman, boy or girl. You looked at white people as trouble. I'm talking about a particular condition that existed in Black America as different from Blacks in the Caribbean Islands and in Africa. They do not recognize it the same way because it is not manifested the same way. The fact that they do not recognize it the same way, is an indication of their political naivete in relationship to white people. That's a big issue!

Finally, in Africa one day, while sitting with some Africans, I saw a white person and I was so secure. For the first time in my life I felt no fear and knew exactly why. I was in a sea of blackness; I was in a sea of security. There was nothing - absolutely nothing - that he could do to me. I didn't resent him because he wasn't to be resented no more than an adult resents a child. Among my experiences, it was a liberating experience.

Now as a teacher, how do you get that across without teaching people to hate. What I am saying is that, how do you get this across, that we are never, absolutely, never to forgive and forget what happened to us; that there is a higher revenge -- short of killing, short of finding a Black branch of the Ku Klux Klan, short of being ridiculous enough to have found a Black Nazi Party -- all of which is a waste of time. Those kinds of things are all a demeaning of our humanity; and yet we must protect ourselves and have no illusions about that. There is a way of doing it without being ridiculous enough to demean our humanity, or without losing our humanity. I learned a lesson from that incident, and I'm glad to have learned the lesson and will never stop appreciating it.

See, I refer to returning to New York as "My Home in Exile" because my historical home is in Africa. If I had any doubts about that, I had none after going to Africa and discovering Africa was my home. Back in the United States, while I waited for the customs officer to finish with the people ahead of me, as he finished with them, he turned to me and said, "You're next boy!" That did it. I was back to the home in exile. That was the signal to let me know that I was back to American reality. "You're next boy!"

A personal friend of mine had paid part of my rent for the big studio I had on 136th Street near Bradhurst, so that I could have it when I got home. Friends cleaned it up, and put up a welcoming sign. I had made up my mind that instead of working and going back to my old job, I would write. And I insisted on telling the African story as I saw it and felt it. This was the book I entitled, *Africa Without Tears*, (as I said earlier on, this book was never published). In the book, I said, "Don't cry for Africa. Forget about Tarzan because he isn't there, and couldn't exist there. If Africans ever found a crazy white man like Tarzan leaping from tree to tree, they would put him out of his misery. Weep for yourself, because Africans have it straight. Don't weep for them. They are more secure than you are. Leave them alone to develop."

I saw Ghana as the political light of the Africa still to be, and I was frightened. I was frightened because I suspected that the colonial powers would not give up Africa very easily, and that the first target of fragmentation would be Ghana. Unfortunately, history proved me right.

In visiting pre-independent Nigeria, I could see that country being set up by the English to fall apart. I saw it as a potential industrial giant; and, I knew it would never make it because of being set up by the English to fall apart. I saw it as a potential industrial giant, and I knew it would never make it because of being set up to fragment within itself.

I came back to the United States to face my problems. I decided that I was going to write. I kept thinking of my daughter I had from the previous relationship that never went quite well, even though I supported the daughter well; and, I wondered if I would make enough money to survive and support her, if I wrote for a living.

Nevertheless, I came back to teach and to write. But the return from home in Africa to my home in exile in the United States was the ending of one aspect of my career and the beginning of another.

John Henrik Clarke: The Early Years

Dr. Clarke pictured
th his sister, Mary in
e living room of her
ɔme in Columbus Geor-
a. Mary's oldest daug-
er, Charlie Mae is in
e background.
:ptember, 1965.

2. Sister Mary; her son,
John Henry Hobbs; and
daughter, Lillie Kate
Hobbs on the front lawn
of her home in Colum-
bus, Georgia. July, 1991.

3. With Cousin Annie Bell Taylor, who was married to L.T. Taylor. September, 1965

4. With Leona Davis, step-mother's sister. Columbus, Georgia. September, 1965

65

John Henrik Clarke: The Early Years

5. Stepsister, Earlene (nicknamed Bit) and oldest child from father's second marriage. January, 1964

6. Ollie Mae Davis and husband, Lawyer Davis with their grandchildren after church in front of Gethsemane Baptist Church. Columbus, Georgia. September, 1965.

John Henrik Clarke: The Early Years

7. The former Fifth Avenue School, which is no longer used as a school, was the first school attended. July, 1991

8. Site of William H. Spencer High School and second school attended, where the 7th grade was located, due to overcrowding in the Fifth Avenue School. July, 1991

9. Former Miller Hills Elementary School, renamed Miller Taylor Elementary School. July, 1991

10. In the home of Elton Motley, in Barbados with novelist Lionel Hutchinson, pictured on the left. January, 1980

11. Elton Motley, host in Barbados. January, 1980

12.With Joyce Motley attending a dinner in his honor in Barbados. January, 1980.

13. Favorite pass-time. Talking and Listening intently to students, during recent visit to Chicago. Fall, 1991

14. Attending City College function. New York, 1988

John Henrik Clarke: The Early Years

15. Speaking at City College function, sponsored by the Department
of Black Studies. New York, 1988

16. Lecturing in Senegal. Summer, 1986

17. Relaxing in museum in Senegal. Summer, 1986.

18. With Professor Leonard Jeffries, Chairman, Department of Black Studies, City College. New York, 1988

19. Pictured with Melvina Hurst prior to lecture, in the lobby of the Manhattan Branch of the New York Urban League. New York, February, 1989

20. Arriving for first Black History Month event presented at the Manhattan Branch of the New York Urban League in Harlem. February, 1989.

21. With Barbara Adams at the League in Harlem. February, 1989.

22. With owners of the celebrated Hot Pot Restaurant, located on 132nd Street and Adam Clayton Powell Boulevard, Harlem, New York. Spring, 1990

3. Visiting with Dr. John Jackson, former teacher and mentor, Chicago, Illinois. Fall, 1991

24. Roscoe Chester, childhood friend since 5th Grade. Columbus, Georgia. July, 1991.

25. Nieces, grand nieces and great grands.
Charlie Mae Rowell, niece (rear left), with her daughters and grandchildren. Columbus, Georgia. July, 1991.

26. Dr. Yosef-ben Joc annan, friend of almo forty years. Taken front of Egyptian Mus um in Cairo, Egyp August, 1991.

John Henrik Clarke: The Early Years

27. Don & Judy Miller who are dear and old friends. Don Miller is the artist who was commissioned by Cornell University to do art work of Dr. Clarke. This display is currently on exhibit at the university. Luxor, Egypt. August, 1991

28. Leaving the Hot Pot Restaurant after lunch with Barbara Adams. Spring, 1990.

29. Barbara Adams with Dr. Yosef ben Jochannan, and Dr. Clarke taken at Convent Avenue Baptist Church on the evening of their join Black History Month presentation. March 4, 1991

30. Black History Month presentation at Abyssinian Baptist Church. February 10, 1992

31. Ariel view of audience attending lecture at Abyssinian Baptist Church February 10, 1992.

Part II

SELECTED LECTURES

*he first Black History Month Lecture by John Henrik :lark, promoted by Barbara Adams for the Manhattan *ranch of the New York Urban League, 204 West 136th :treet, in Harlem, February 22, 1989.*

CAN WE SAVE HARLEM?

I could ask and answer the question in short order, and we could all go home, but that would serve no purpose. As to, can we save Harlem; maybe, depending on what kind of political forces we put together.

I find it interesting, now that that we stand a chance of losing this community, we are just beginning to gain some interest in it. What I'm going to be talking about is how Harlem became a Black community in the first place and what we can do, if anything, to save this community.

The new interest in Harlem is centered on new interest in Adam Powell, our best politician and new interest in Malcolm X, who used Harlem as a proving ground for leadership. The new interest is around the question -- *If we lose Harlem, where are we going?* Those who want to take Harlem, don't care where we are going.

There was a plan that came from the Housing Authority about thirty years ago called "Planned Shrinkage." It was a deliberate plan to shrink the housing accommodation in

New York, to drive out not just the Black poor, but the white poor also.

The people who take the Long Island Railroad were growing tired of the breakdowns, the snowfalls and the holdups. They wanted to move closer to their jobs. They wanted to make New York City the bedroom community, and the suburbs would become the outer slum community or the servants' quarters. Powerful multi-million dollar real estate interests are involved here. And, you dare not mention another ethnic group when they unite against us, because they're going to hide behind something called "minority" and you're going to become "anti-something" for reminding them that they too are a part of the totality of oppression. See we're in a bind; it is a cultural bind, a political bind, and a religious bind.

I do not usually deal with the religious aspect because some Blacks will kill you for dealing with it. We are trapped by a book; a great book of knowledge, a book of lessons, a book of folklore (not history) called the Bible. We're trapped by a Jewish survival book and a very good Jewish survival book that they strategically use and throw away when they want to. But we keep it all the way. We don't use it strategically, we surely don't use it academically, because it is a great resource. It is basically folklore told to illustrate the truth many times, and we hink when something illustrates the truth that the illustration must also be true. See, we are trapped by someone else's folklore, someone else's interpretation and we forget that the interpretation is a carbon copy of a far greater interpretation that we had before the first European wore a shoe and lived in a house with a window.

This is what we will not deal with. We will not deal with our origins in history. If we dealt with our origins in history, then we could deliver the right message to ourselves. Now, what has this got to do with, "Can we save Harlem?" I say everything, because we can't save anything until we have enough confidence to do it.

It was only two hundred years ago, when we didn't have a good wheelbarrel. So why do we have so much today? The answer is the restoration of self confidence; to go out into the world so that the people who oppressed us, and the people who humiliated us, cannot do a single thing that we can't. If a human mind can do it, then we can do it.

Why is there so much mystery in building a train? To make ten trains, all you need is one. To make ten watches, all you need is one watch, break it down and assign each part to one person. You don't even have to put the burden on one lone human being. Joe can make the hands, you can make the wheels, another can make the casing, someone else, the stem; put it all together and you have a watch.

What has happened to us that we do not understand that we can save not only this community, but also every community where we live? A community is a miniature nation and we can rehearse for the ruling of a nation by the control of a community.

We have to go back and read people that we have not properly considered in spite of the years they preached and the years their philosophy has been available to us. We must go back and really look at Booker T. Washington, W.E.B. DuBois, Marcus Garvey, Malcolm X, and the Nation's concept of Elijah Muhammad. When you lose the concept of belonging to something called a "nation," you not only can't save a community, you can't save yourselves. When you're locked into someone else's culture to the point where you don't even know your actual name, and answer to names you did not invent and pray to a god you did not assign to yourself, other people do not have to build a prison wall for you because you're behind a much bigger wall built by yourself.

If we're going to save this community, we're going to have to look at the program of self reliance as advocated by Washington. If you live in a brick house, what's wrong with owning a brick yard? If you wear leather shoes, what's wrong with being a leather tanner? What's wrong with supporting every element of all the things that you need to sustain yourself in the society where you live? If you maintain yourself in the society where you live, if you maintain a community, then you can maintain a nation, because the maintenance of a community is rehearsal for the maintenance of a nation. If we stand a chance of losing this community, it is because we have not martialled the political forces, the technical forces, the basic know how, the educational system, all necessary to maintain a nation. So if we had that apparatus intact, and if we had the community politically intact, we could save Harlem politically and educationally. We cannot have it just one way. We have to look at DuBois again, we have to stop assuming that there was a fight between DuBois and Washington. There was a difference of opinion between the two. If you want to identify someone who had a fight with Booker T. Washington, it was William Monroe Trotter, the Boston Bomber Editor, of the famous Guardian Newspaper. Now, there was a fight! DuBois and Washington had a difference of opinion and, yet, they worked together. Few people seemed to know that DuBois and Washington wrote two books together, mostly on education. The books are still available. These men were not enemies. So it was not a problem of choosing between DuBois or Booker T. Washington then or now. Right now, we see it as a problem of following DuBois or Booker T. Washington because both of them were right. Washington was right in his educational ap-

proach and weak in his political approach. DuBois wa
right in his political approach and a little premature based
on where we were at that time.

Once you get a house and get a job in a national
community, you automatically become political because
you want to protect it. DuBois wanted it at once, but
Washington wanted us to go through a process and arrive
as if political. So this was not a fight, it was just a choice of
priorities and where we needed to go. This so-called fight
between DuBois, Washington and Garvey was another
misunderstanding, or another non-fight, classified as a
fight.

I'm starting this way because there was something at the
beginning of this century we couldn't settle, and it was at
the beginning of this century that we began to take over
this community called Harlem.

Harlem is unique in Black communities. It is unique in
Black communities because it's on the other side of
nothing. Harlem is the geographic heart of New York City.
The ventilation of Harlem is better than other parts of the
city. Harlem is situated between the rivers, and gets a finer
grade of air considering the lowness of buildings. That is,
until they built that monstrosity at City College -- now,
there's a wind breaker! The wind coming from both sides
of the river would hit Harlem with equal balance before
they built that wind breaker. Harlem is in the best part of

New York from a point of view of transportation. The transportation arteries that run through Harlem connect with the total of New York City and when you're in Harlem, there are very few places in Manhattan that you can't reach within a half hour. Harlem is very convenient to get to, very convenient to get back to, and convenient to move from. So it is clear that they did not build this community for us and that we got the community by default.

When they first built Harlem, the ads for apartments said "from your apartment to Wall Street in 27 minutes" and that was when they began to extend the subway. I timed it in the years when I used to go to New York University before they threw me out for criticizing them on the way they were teaching white history. They insulted me with the inept way they were teaching history. And I didn't expect them to teach Black History at all.

Now, I lived at Bradhurst and 136th Street. Bradhurst Avenue went down to 136th Street in those days. From my door to sitting down in the classroom, if I made the right subway connection, it took me 27 minutes. Now that's convenience, and it's not like going to Long Island where you have to wait on the train. And, then when you get to the end of your ride, if your car is not there to pick you up, you have to take a taxi because there's no bus service running along those suburbs.

With Blacks coming to Harlem, the whites began to panic because they saw a few of us. A brilliant real estate man, called Proctor, invented something called "block busting," by moving some Blacks into one block. Whites panicked and moved out. He moved others in until we gradually had the community. There is much more to it than that because there was an aristocratic element that came to Harlem. Aristocratic is the wrong word, and middle class is also the wrong word, and I don't really like the word middle class as applied to Black people because I don't understand, middle from what? To have a middle, you've got to have an upper and I haven't located the upper. I'd like to think of a responsible class because Harlem once had a responsible class. At least, we could pick up the telephone and get the streets cleaned. There was a period when they didn't even have time to get dirty. When I came to Harlem, I could lay down in the streets because they were so clean. They were clean and safe too. I could walk around at midnight and argue with roustabouts. All-night restaurants were open with good food. I just loved this place.

Coming out of the South where I couldn't even use the public library, I now had a place where I could go in and check out six books, and read them and come back and check out six more. This made me go hog wild. It was a ew haven and heaven too. See, I have never lived more than a one-mile radius from 135th Street in the fifty-five years I've been here. I didn't plan it that way, but I always wanted to be close to the library because that was my university without tuition. I have used it well. That block at 135th Street between Lenox and Seventh Avenue, close to the Schomburg Collection, of the public library, is where I went to the Harlem History Clubs of the 1930's. It was there under the tutelage of Dr. Willis N. Huggins, that I earned the political meaning of history. Down the street from the Schomburg, I learned the interrelationship of our history to the world.

From the lectures of William Leo Hansberry of Howard University, I learned the philosophical meaning of history. And I learned about the African contribution of the brotherhood of man and humanity from Seifort.

Taking a kid, such as myself, out of the South and training him by the great Black master teachers was an unbeatable combination. Now, I don't just know history from one angle, I've learned it from all these different angles. And, none of the teachers charged me anything for their services; they were glad to teach me. You don't find students that way anymore and you don't find teachers that way anymore either.

All right, let me begin the lecture that's going to be brief anyway. Around 1527, when this was a Dutch Colony, about twenty Africans landed. They, like the Africans who landed in Jamestown in 1619, were indentured slaves rather than chattel slaves. Chattel slavery did not exist all over the Americas. Let me make a clear distinction between chattel slaves and indentured slaves. Indentured slaves work for many years and are then freed. The chattel slave is enslaved to the end of his days.

The Catholic Church (the whole idea was picked up by the British later) started chattel slavery, where if you were a slave, you were never able to get out of it. Most chattel slavery started on the island of Hispaniola, now Haiti and Santo Domingo, and is recorded in the works of Father Bartholomé de las Casas in a famous book called *The Destruction of the Indies*. He is the first historian of the New World. His book was so devastating that the Pope had it sent to Rome, locked it up and for two hundred years, no one was able to read it. You can now only get it in a very good library, and even in a very good library, the librarian is going to look at you with suspicion, because it tells of the systematic destruction of the indigenous Americans who were mistakenly called Indians, because Christopher Columbus ended up on the wrong side of the world. Starting for the East Indies but ending up in the West Indies, he slapped the word Indian on the people. Because of the destruction of these people, a petition went to Rome to increase the African slave trade. With the consequence of this increase, the Dutch began to import Africans; but mostly on an indentured basis. These were captured Africans who were enslaved, but enslaved in a different way.

It would be good to read the work by Father de las Casas through someday, if you can live through the suspicious stare of the librarian. This book is still widely circulated. There are many books about him, but before you read about him, read what he said, then read Christopher Columbus' diary. I won't dwell on this long because Columbus is my favorite antihero. I think he was one of the great frauds of human history who discovered absolutely nothing.

Now, the Dutch established themselves in what they called New Amsterdam, New York's Manhattan Island. I won't get into this whole nonsense about the Indians selling the Island for $24.00; let's stop insulting the Indians with that nonsense. If you understand indigenous cultures of people, you will understand that people gave permission to use the land based on the concept that it would be used properly, not used against their people. Otherwise, they would take it back. And so when land was exchanged, the token gift was not a purchase price but a pledge of assurance that the land would be properly used and would not be used against those who gave permission to use the land. If you study old treaties, you would find this occurring again and again, because the concept of will, the concept of land, the concept of deed, all these are Western things that the people refused to deal with. Don't think that all of these concepts have been here forever. Wills, deeds, and legal documents have not been here forever.

Look, when I was a Sergeant Major in the Army, I had to handle administrative things and divorces. I discovered something that still prevails in some quarters today, namely the concept of divorce was alien to our culture because no one had ever had one. The idea of jail wasn't part of our language because no one had ever been to one. The idea of old peoples' homes wasn't part of our language either because no one had ever thrown away grandma and grandpa. The idea of an orphanage was also alien to our language because we weren't giving away our children. If a child had no mother or father, someone in the family, or someone in the community would take him in and give him shelter. It was not a matter of adoption, or a matter of looking for a home, it was an automatic process. We came out of a society where we incubated in a culture container, alien to the one they brought us into and we developed certain basic traits in the Western world that we did not have before we got here. We became a whole lot of things here that we were not, because the slave ships did not bring any West Indians or East Indians.

We did not come as Deltas, or AKA's, or Elks. There weren't any high yellas, and people with a gender problem. The one thing that God, in his infinite genius, designed was a woman that was super special and we had no conflict within ourselves about who we needed to be affectionate toward. All this other mixup we took on, was somebody else's culture and somebody else's alienation.

A few months ago I delivered a lecture to a Black sorority on "Historical Origins of Black Teenage Pregnancy." They were so disappointed that they didn't even send me the small honorarium for the lecture. I lectured for an hour and ten minutes and didn't blame the Black man for nothing. They were all sitting there waiting for me to castrate the brother from head to toe, and I just left him out. There's no teenage pregnancy in Africa, no one slapping women around in Africa. I didn't have time to condemn the Black man, and that's what they came to hear me do.

Back to New Amsterdam; these few Africans found a home in a place called Chatham Square, now Chinatown. They were basically servants, who were thrown out by other immigrant groups. They moved a little further uptown to Washington Square which had been their burial ground.

A swamp called Greenwich Village, that no one could drain, was given to the Blacks. Now eat your heart out, and think about real estate prices now. We once owned Greenwich Village, and we got it for nothing because nobody else wanted it. And so we began to build communities there. There's no indication that the early Africans brought any women, but a generation later they were marrying and putting up a semblance of family. We can assume that they married Dutch women. We can also assume that because no one was kicking, screaming, and hollering rape, there was no objection. I cannot recollect anything to the contrary. We forget that color prejudice had a hard time getting started because poor whites had not been convinced that there was any difference between their lot and our lot. When we arrived in 1619, most of the indentured slaves were white and there was no conflict between them and the Africans. They were catching the same hell from the same masters.

If you want a capsule history of this, Lerone Bennett has written an excellent work called *The Shaping of Black America*. The first chapter is called "White Servitude," the second chapter is called "First Generation" dealing with the first generation of Africans. If you want a capsule history of the Africans on Manhattan Island, there's another excellent and popular book called *New World a Coming*. I'm not bringing anything to you out of the sky. James Weldon Johnson also wrote an excellent book called *Dark Manhattan*. There's a whole segment of literature on this subject, and I didn't write all of it, just some of it.

These Africans in Lower Manhattan worked their way out of indenture by building a wagon road from Lower Manhattan to a Dutch Farm in Upper Manhattan called Harlem. They didn't live near the place because this was an aristocratic Dutch community that rich Dutch farmers had. Alexander Hamilton had a house that's still on Convent Avenue. He was the first Secretary of the Treasury whose life is a mystery because people don't want to admit that his mother came from Nieves, that she was Black and his father was otherwise. And, so he had more than the one drop, which made him a whole one of us. Digging up this kind of information and smearing it in peoples' faces doesn't mean that they get the point.

We worked our way out of indenture, but we still needed a community. We began to go further uptown. Pressure would come from the Irish community that would last a hundred years. These were the Irish Black wars. They are well recorded. And someone asked me, "Inasmuch as you know so much about it, and talk so much about it, why don't you write a book on the Irish Black Wars?" I said, "One day when I am silly enough to recognize something called old, and I have run out of things to do, I might write a history of these wars." I am not anxious to do this because we lost. We lost the wars. After Tammany

Hall was created, the Irish got off of our backs and built one of the most colorful and corrupt political machines ever imagined. There is plenty of history on Tammany Hall, but very few tell the truth about the absolute corruption of Tammany Hall.

Africans moved into a neighborhood around 29th and 30th Streets, until they demolished that neighborhood to build Pennsylvania Station and the main post office. This was the first Black Urban Renewal Removal Program that I know about. We began to move further uptown to the 50's and 60's on the West Side. The Africans who went to the Spanish American War came back to this area. Many of them did not go to their homes in the South because they had to fight to hold onto the community.

Our first actors, and producers thrived in this vicinity. Marion Cook, father of Mercer Cook who was head of Romance Languages at Howard University, came from this area. He's dead now. He married the famous teenage singer Abby Mitchell, a legendary singer in her day. Abby Mitchell's daughter married a famous vaudevillian who was a rage in Europe, but couldn't get his career off of the ground in the United States.

There was a time before Nazism, when Blacks used to go to Germany to appear in movies. Blacks had the success in Europe that they couldn't achieve in the United States. Marion Cook came back from Europe with all his musical training and wanted to write for the Metropolitan Opera. He was qualified, but they told him that they didn't want any coon writers for the Metropolitan Opera. Marion Cook started listening to the voices of Black people which he used to compose and set what he heard to music. Later he made a fair reputation for himself as the forerunner of the musical comedy that was copied, modeled and revolutionalized by whites in their musical comedies.

There also appeared a great Caribbean figure during this early period named Bert Williams. He became one of the greatest single comedians ever produced in this country. Few people know that he was from Antigua. He was trained in England by the same pantominist as Charlie Chaplin. He was a trained Shakespearean and he came to this country and wanted to do Shakespeare. White folks laughed at him. They said, "Give me a coon show and I'll listen to you." And so he learned Black dialect; he learned stories of the landlord; he learned about the sisters in the church and became one of the most able of comedians and entertainers. Perhaps Bert Williams was the greatest Black entertainer we've ever produced in America. He was never vulgar maybe spicy, but never vulgar. You take the Murphys and the Pryors, they're just down right filthy and vulgar.

Now, let me give you an example of what I'm talking about, then I'll go into history. I got this from one of Bert

Williams' notebooks which is housed in the Schomburg Collection. The Schomburg has many humorous works if you just ask for them. One of his famous church jokes was about a lady who said, "Last night I slept in the arms of sin, but now I've seen the way of the Lord and tonight I'm going to sleep in the arms of Jesus." And some evil brother tapped her on the shoulder and said, "Hey sister, how are you fixed for tomorrow night?" If you have the time some day, go to the Schomburg and read Bert's notebooks. Now what has this got to do with history? It has a lot. It was the Bert Williams' type, the Marion Cook's type, the James Weldon Johnson's type that began to buy houses at 139th Street and they had to strive to pay the rent. Whites charged them so much extra for the houses that they had to strive real hard to keep up the payments. Now, how was it named Striver's Row? We were charged the astronomical sum of $10,000 for a little old house. That was a big price in that day. Those same houses are now selling for a quarter million dollars, although they were built for about $7,000. Labor was cheap and good, material was good and not too expensive. Many of the garages there used to be carriage houses for their horses. So we began to move into an aristocratic neighborhood.

Now, the moving into 133rd Street and the Block Busting had already occurred. This was one level of Blacks moving into Harlem.

From them, you had a level of Blacks moving into Harlem who were going to be the responsible people in the future. The responsible elite, not middle class, just responsible people. With them, you now had the formation of political parties. There was a brilliant Black bellhop named Ed Lee who was the bellhop at the old Warwick Hotel where Tammany Hall's bigwigs went for extracurricular activity, not necessarily with their wives. He had the dirt on all of them. He knew what kind of liquor they drank; and he knew the color of the hair of their respective mistresses. And, so when he asked the head of Tammany Hall to give him money to open up a Government Branch Office, the Tammany Hall's boss said, "I will not only give you the money, but I will put a Negro in every Branch of the Government." This was one of the few promises that was ever made to us that was almost kept. Almost kept. I mean, we didn't have inspectors, we had people in the courts. Although we didn't have any judges, we had court personnel. Those were jobs. They were steady, and gave you a little pension at the end. It wasn't so bad, and the health services were pretty good. So we began to get these things thanks to Ed Lee.

The Republicans made a bid under the leadership of Charlie Anderson. He was a great authority on taxes. After Ed Lee, we had formed a Black Branch within the Democratic Party called the United Colored Democracy.

Charlie Anderson became a collector for the Internal Revenue Service from the first district in Wall Street. We were moving up then, thanks to a common ordinary bellhop finding a political organization that related to the totality of people, not just to the elitist form of the people. Finally, pushing into the 20's, we became tired of the little plums and wanted some bigger plums, so we went to our respective political parties and demanded a Black judge. Each party told us that we were crazy; that we didn't have a Black who had enough sense to judge anything. They told us to find two qualified ones and they would be considered. So we found two qualified men, one whose name was Watson who had come from the Caribbean Islands. He had seen Black judges before; Black constables, school masters and Black administrators. These were jobs that the English were too lazy to keep, and so they gave them to us. We had the false illusion that they were giving the positions to us because they liked us. The judgeship didn't present a problem to Watson; he accepted it. The other candidate didn't even believe it. He went down to North Carolina to visit his mother. When he finally reported to work, we had two judges.

In the midst of this, a literary movement called the Harlem Renaissance was developed. It was tapered off in the 1930's. It was in the 1930's that whites began to lose their money and they stopped coming to Harlem looking or noble savage or the exotic Negro. Many unemployed and college trained Blacks could see that whites were losing money. These Blacks became known as unemployed professionals; and, they told gullible whites about art inside of their soul, and novels still to be published, if only they had some money. And the whites gave them money. These were actors, and good ones. But, whatever they did, they contributed to our upward mobility and our clarification. They also proved that in a social situation they could be just as big a snob as any white person. They could balance a cocktail glass with the best of them; and, they could say vichyssoise as if they never heard of a pork chop. We thank them for their contribution.

It was a period of production; it was a period of the outpouring of great literature. Harlem became literally the Mecca for night clubs, and a lot of original plays were launched here.

When I arrived in 1933, there wasn't a single boarded up house in all of the community. The community was flourishing, it was well kept and things were moving. But the trouble of the depression got its emphasis from the Harlem riot of 1935. Out of this riot would come the beginning of the career of Adam Clayton Powell who was an Assistant Pastor and would later become Pastor of Abyssinian Baptist Church. He would use Abyssinian Baptist Church very strategically. Anyone who had a meeting could meet in the church. People involved in peace movements would meet in the church. Some of the great peace songs were introduced in the church; and, a lot of people who played a role are still alive today.

The famous river to river picket line down 125th Street happened then. It would seem inconceivable to your generation that there was a time when Blacks didn't even have clerk jobs on 125th Street. There was a store called Weisbeckers where we had to picket just to get Blacks in them. And once Blacks were hired, they became so snobbish and offensive, we wanted to put another picket line together to get them out. They didn't know how to handle power.

Then we began to boycott the telephone company. Some meter readers were hired, but the telephone company would not hire female operators. This was before the dial telephone; when you picked up the phone and someone said, "number, please" like the white operators. On a business level, we had good relationships with some communists who had jobs at the telephone company. So we had them train some of the Black girls on how to speak this phony telephone language. The communists put Blacks behind a screen where whites couldn't see them and the whites couldn't distinguish between the Black girls and the white girls. But Blacks could distinguish the Black girls because the Black girls poke that phony language far better than the whites. So Blacks got these jobs and we began to try to launch better campaigns like, "Don't buy where you can't work." I'm speaking about this because I arrived here in time to participate in this kind of activity. Adam Clayton Powell became part of the Coordinated Committee for Negro Employment. That was the beginning of his political career and it was sanctioned by the father of the movement of that day, A. Philip Randolph. We still had the community intact and it was still our community.

Adam Powell continued to be active and visible in the political movement to get jobs for Blacks on 125th Street. He was also successful in getting Blacks hired as bus drivers. When there was an opening in the City Council, he ran and was elected to the office. That was literally his launching pad. The Harlem community became his window on the world. Later on, he was active on the broader political scene. The old Harlem History Club developed at the Harlem Y, and many notable people came to that club and received training. Among those coming to the club, was a student from Lincoln University named Francis K. Nkrumah, who was later known as Kwame. The great white pacifist, John Haynes Holmes, spoke at the club. Willis Huggins designed a concept that would later be called Black Studies right there in the chapel of the Harlem Y. Huggins, also, authored *The Guide* to the *Study of African History* and *An Introduction to African History.*

John Jackson began his early writings in association with the club. His works included: *The Origins of the Legends of the Garden of Eden, Was Jesus Christ a Negro, Pagan Origins of the Christ Myth,* and *Christianity Before Christ.* His writings which dealt with elements that went into the making of Islam, Christianity and Judaism before Christ, were all the outcome of the Harlem History Club.

I've celebrated John Jackson's 79th birthday three times, and I'm assuming he is about 83. He says he's 79 and holding. Every time John has a serious illness, he calls people in to write his obituary and tells us "to carry on in his name," and that he took the struggle as far as he could. He also tells us to remember him. John Jackson will probably live another ten years. He recently finished what he calls his "magnum opus," "his supreme work." It is not just the history of the world, but the history of the whole world. John Jackson has left us with what he calls his masterpiece, "his crowning glory." Everyone should live long enough to write the book he considers his supreme effort.

He has been ill, but he's back home now and is partially recovered. He says that medicine keeps him alive. When I visited him last year, he had already requested that his body be given to science. I told him that, scientifically, his ody wasn't even worth 80¢ because everything was gone and broken down.

My main point, and I am about to conclude, is that Harlem became the proving ground for men and movements who tried to make it in Harlem. If they didn't make it in Harlem, then, they didn't make it elsewhere. There were great religious movements that came before Father Divine; but, Father Divine benefited and flourished in the community because his housing program and his restaurant program fed a whole lot of us when we had nowhere else to turn. Other movements were the Elijah Muhammad Movement, the Resurgence of the Garvey Movement, and the World Federation for Ethiopia Movement after the Italian-Ethiopian War.

I am saying that we have produced here, one of the most unique African Communities in the world, where early rich Black women like Madam Walker and her daughter hung out. Josephine Baker visited Harlem before she went to Paris, got lost and came back to America pretending she couldn't speak English. They were all Harlem's products, and they all came back to the magnet.

I was in Northern Nigeria years ago and didn't think anyone knew me or Harlem, when someone hollered out, "say American, you from Harlem?" So Harlem is known around the world. The Black community in Rome is composed mostly of Somalian people, and that section is called Little Harlem. So the word Harlem is universal. It conjures up more than just a community. It conjures up a culture because a culture unfolded in this community -- a very unique culture. A literature was produced about the community and around the community and by community residents.

I hope we can hold onto this community. If we are to hold onto it, we must hold onto it politically. We must not only challenge the political rulers of the community, we must challenge those who represent us, and if they cannot help us save this community, then we must show them that we can replace them.

My answer to "Can we save the Harlem community?" is that we better save the Harlem community. I have lived here for most of my life, and happen to be a minor property owner in this community. I will put my bid in first in the effort to save the community. And since we can do it, we must do it because we have no other community that would welcome us. We have no other community that has the same memories for so many different people. Yes, we will save it. It will not be easy, but we must train ourselves that this community is part of the semblance of a nation among African people. And once we get back the concept of nation structure and nation management, the saving of the Harlem community will be less difficult for us. We must not only challenge its educational system, we must challenge its political system and when we claim it, we're going to have to clean it up and make it the dream community that it once was and must be again!

Thank you very much.

Kwanza Lecture by Prof. John Henrik Clarke, promoted by Barbara Adams for the Manhattan Branch of the New York Urban League, and hosted by Gramham/Windham Manhattan Center in Harlem, December 19, 1990.

CEREMONY AND CELEBRATION IN AFRICAN SOCIETY

Once we as a people find ourselves on the map of human geography and find the kind of clock we need to tell time by -- the cultural clock, the political clock and the historical clock. And, once we stop trying to be like other people and celebrate the fact that we are different and being different has helped us survive; then, we will understand that we came out of a different kind of structured society and a different kind of structured spirituality. We will understand that in this society, our emphasis was not on religion, but rather on spirituality; and, spirituality is higher than religion. The African recognized and honored the force of nature and the force of the universe, which made him different from the European who tried to defy nature. The African tried to bring humankind in harmony with nature. He tried to make man understand that he must flow and move with the seasons; that he could not fight the wind, the forces or the universe. So everything in life became a part of the

otality of his spirituality and his God force or spiritual
orce.

During most of the existence of man on the face of the
earth, the word G-O-D was not a part of the vocabulary of
any people. Most people who are spiritual and use the
word religion, do not use the word G-O-D. I am not saying
that they are godless. Each man and each culture chooses
a word for God that reflects its meaning in the culture for
which it was produced. He is not spiritual or religious
because of it; he has chosen a word and an image of the
deity that reflects who he is and who-so-ever God is. He is
not less because some Africàns call him Shàngó, and some
Arabs call him Allah and some other Africans call him
Olódùmarè. He is not less.

Now with the coming of the European to power in the
world, because of his sickness and insecurity, not only
Africa ran into trouble, but the world found itself in
trouble to the extent that we left the cultural base of our
creation and became an imitator of someone else's
concept of culture.

Now, let's tell about how the Africans, the Asians and
people in warmer climates celebrated the force of nature
and how the Europeans tried to fight the force of nature.
In Europe, nature was unkind. There was all that snow for
three or four months which did not allow enough time to
plant, to harvest and to store. And so, the European was

angry with nature for not giving him enough time to survive. But, in Africa, nature is kind and sends fruits and vegetables every season. In Africa, nature also sends fish all year round; while in Europe, the ponds are frozen and there is a limited time when you can fish or store.

So the Europeans developed an attitude toward nature that is deviant, while the African, and other people in warmer climates developed an attitude toward nature that made them celebrate the bountifulness of nature. The African would celebrate the harvest all year round. He would celebrate birth, and he would celebrate death as a continuation of life. He was a total spiritual human being. He did not lose this spirituality until he came in touch with foreigners who misinterpreted his spirituality, formalized it, dogmatized it, put it into books called the Bible and put that word on it as though there was no other book worthy of being called the Bible. "The," the only one. Either this one or no one. And yet, the one he composed had curses in it, and had the dogma of great teaching, but always mixed with conflict. You will find that if you read certain portions of the Bible, there is just as much conflict in it as in a detective story.

If you read the literature created in Africa before the creation of the Bible, you will find that the African drew from man and he drew from spirit. He drew from man's experience, the know-how of survival. The first thing, the

African tried to establish were the taboos, what not to do. Once you are clear on what not to do, by a process of elimination, you know what to do, which would eventually emerge in the world as civil law. This happened long before 2000 BC when the so-called law that was used as the basis of Western Law and lacked humanity was announced. So in the beginning of Western Law, there was a lack of recognition of the human beginnings of a human being. And when these foreigners misinterpreted the spirituality of non-European people, formalized it into dogma and called it a religion, they turned one religion into another and made all organized Western religions male chauvinist, murder cults. Name me the religion, and I will describe the murder cult and the male chauvinistic aspect of that religion.

What I'm trying to say is that we celebrate life because nature gave us something to celebrate. We celebrate harvest because we have food. The reason the European did not celebrate life was because nature was so stingy, not giving him enough to eat, not giving him enough women to procreate with and not giving him enough land to raise enough food. All this made him angry with nature. On the other hand, Africans had plenty of all of this. The African could celebrate the kindness of nature, he could celebrate birth, he could celebrate marriage, he could celebrate manhood, he could celebrate moving from one status to another, he could celebrate eldership, he could celebrate the fact that someone had grown old and by virtue of growing old he had accumulated wisdom. He could celebrate grandma, he could celebrate grandpa Mind you, we have not lost all of this celebration of old people and the use of the aged. When we came to the United States, we lost a lot of it and almost all of it now, but I grew up in an environment where we celebrated our elders.

My great Grandmother, Ma Mary, was literally the Supreme Court and when she announced her decision or when there was a shadow of a doubt that her decision was going to be accepted she would just stand up and tap her cane on the floor. That was all, there was no reprieve. Grandma had spoken. When one of the members of the family brought a man in and introduced him to Grandma, Grandma looked him over. Now mind you, when Grandma made a decision, sometimes it was good, sometimes it was bad, and sometimes it broke the girl's heart, but it kept her safe. Grandma's decision wasn't always pretty. Sometimes she'd say, "Gal, get rid of that man, keep your dress tail down; don't give him nothing, get rid of him." There wasn't a debate about it. She didn't want him in the family, and almost all of the uncles, mostly her sons, would back her up. That was the end of it.

Having lived in and among a number of African societies

cluding the Ga and the Ewe in West Africa, the Akan in hana, and the Yoruba and the Igbo, I know the one thing at has kept Africans alive is their relationship to nature at you would refer to as God. The African believes in the otality of nature, the wind, the rain and the giver. The African does not believe in anything as being nsignificant; everything has a reason. There are times in a ociety when you have to be removed from it, and you lose our understanding of it. Back in 1958, when Ghana was celebrating the beginning of its independence and Nigeria was expected to be the next big nation to move into the ndependence arena, I began to learn something about the definition of an African culture.

I lived on the outskirts of the city of Accra in Jamestown which was a community mostly for the Ga people. One day when I came back to the family compound, I noticed that there was sadness among the fourteen families living in the compound, but there was no mourning. I knew that a bus driver had been in the hospital and that they expected him to die. I could tell by the atmosphere that he had passed, yet there was no mourning and finally, I learned that his death was not official until the oldest member in the family announced the death. When the death was announced, then the mourning started. that's the sad part of the wake. And I noticed that every time that the widow weeped, women of her age group wept with her. They stopped when she stopped, they consoled her, and she was never alone. Her humanity was respected. Now in the midst of all of this, I fell asleep. When I woke up, the courtyard was full of lights. They were about to celebrate the good life of the deceased, and people were going to give testimony.

One African musician with an ordinary carpenter's saw was making music more beautiful than I've ever heard come from a saw. And, there were all kinds of homemade instruments in the courtyard. Everyone was dancing out his/her relationship to the deceased. Finally, it came my time to dance and I panicked, because I violated the stereotype about Black people being good dancers. So I turned to an African woman and asked,"Where do you put your feet? How do you do the dance?" She said, with a straight face, "Mr. Clarke, you have no feet, it's about the soul. If you remember what the man was to you and how he related to you, then you will dance out the meaning of that relationship, and those things you call your feet will be taken care of because you will be dancing with your heart instead of your feet." For the first time in my life, and with total abandonment as if I was floating in air, I did an African dance exceptionally well. I danced out my relationship to the deceased. I noticed that the wives of the mourners who were mourning with her, danced with her. And that, in celebration of the life of the deceased they danced out the history of that particular group.

On their way home from the burial, there's another dance where each woman takes off one garment and throws it down for her favorite man to dance on. It is a beautiful dance and after he has danced on her garment, she joins in the dance.

As I continued to watch this wake in Ghana, which was a learning experience for me, I saw something at the burial that shocked me. There were seventy-five professional mourners dressed in mourning clothes. Since I remembered that this man was a bus driver, I asked how much did this funeral cost and was told that it cost nothing. There was singing and dancing with the orchestra on the way to the graveyard. The male mourners took the coffin out of the hearse and carried it on their shoulders, while other men and musicians danced on their way to the grave. I would later observe this in New Orleans, and this funeral celebration in New Orleans is still being practiced. The only difference in New Orleans to Africa is that in New Orleans, they dance forward pigeon toe and in Africa, they dance forward slough foot. Same dance, just a different way of holding your feet while celebrating the good life of the deceased, and celebrating that the deceased will now go to a higher life.

On the way back from the funeral, men pass through the streets with big sheets and different people threw money in the sheets. When we finally got back and counted all of the money taken up, it was the equivalent of $6,000. All this is taken by the elders of the family who make sure that it is secure for the widow. The widow spends the next six weeks at the home of the elders, and when she comes home all the clothes she wore when her husband was alive have been disposed of and her house has been cleaned from top to bottom. I have seen this same kind of thing happen in Alabama and Georgia, where I grew up. It happened to the extent that when a house is dirty, there is a sick comment made like, "Why doesn't someone die in the house so it can get really clean." This is said because when there's death in the family, everyone knows that the neighbors come in and clean the house.

Later, the ladies welcomed her back to her neighborhood with her new dress on and the women sang, "As long as there are clothes among your people, you will have clothes." Then the men made her new sandals and sang, "So long as there are shoes among your people, you will have shoes." And they cooked a feast, and all the women whose dish she did not taste felt insulted. So she made a special point of taking a pinch of all the dishes laid before her, and once this was finished, the song says, "As long as there's food among your people you will have food." And the men threw some of the best food on the ground and danced on it giving the assurance that she vould not starve.

I later learned that the best way to spoil the dance was o research it. Some fools called anthropologists looked at :his and called it primitive. This is social security built into a :ulture and this is high civilization. The widow will not have to go to a welfare office to be insulted by some clerk who thinks the money belongs to them. She will not have to borrow and scrape and ask someone to please give her an allowance to buy shirts for little Willie so he can go to school. He will not have to be called a parasite on the community. The uncles, the aunts, everyone will look after her. It is clearly understood that the older brother or the younger brother will take responsibility for her until she has relocated. She won't have to go over to the older brother or younger brother and ask her brother's wife to take care of her younguns, because it will be done already. And the uncles never tell her what they are going to do to help. They just come and help; take her for a walk and ask, "How are things going? Are the school fees paid for the boys or girls?" She lets them know her condition, but never says, "Are you going to give me some money?" And the uncles just take the money out of their pockets while they are walking, and either slip it into her hands, or if she has a breast pocket, then they slip it into that pocket, wish her well, and say, "Call us when you need us." And they're gone. No one has bad mouthed anyone, and no one says,

"Look what I've done for you!" or "You low-down this or
that!" It's built into the culture itself because they're still
celebrating life by maintaining life on this earth. These are
the kinds of things we've lost in part, but not entirely.

My point is that, in a wake, the people remind
themselves of their heroic moment in history. They use this
as a way to celebrate survival, and as they are celebrating
the good life of the deceased who has left them, they also
celebrate their prowess in military matters that kept them
victorious over a people who tried to interfere with their
sovereignty.

I think that E. Franklin Frazier misinterpreted our life
from this point and so did Melvile J. Herskovits in his *Myth
of the Negro Past*. We have to study the people who
studied us and see where they went wrong that the main
place where they went wrong is that they do not
understand that spirituality was part of our totality. This is
why we celebrated the beginning of harvest, the planting
of the vegetables, the harvesting of the food, the end of
the season, both renewal and manhood. You did not
become a man in that society without a ceremony saying
that you were a man. In our society (and forgive the
crudeness), we think that the minute you can get an
erection, that you are a man. You are not a man until you
can be responsible. This is why, in many African societies,
the boys are taken away from the women when they are

about ten, for years of training with the men. If it's a hunting society, he becomes a master hunter. If it's a farming society, he becomes a farmer. He becomes whatever he needs to become, in order to sustain a family, not just to create a family. He learns how to protect a family and how to make his family relate to others so that a series of families can become a village.

Foreigners did not understand that then, and do not understand it now. What we need to do is to go back and look at the Nile Valley of cultural formations, because many times we have over-studied Nile Valley civilization to the neglect of Niger Valley civilization. We must study the similarities of African civilizations on these other rivers and we should read the thoroughness as against gossip about the cultural unity of Black Africa. Where the Africans differ from one part of Africa to the other, is that, there was a sameness in the totality of Black culture until foreigners from Western Asia began to impinge on African culture around 1675 BC.

These foreigners would continue to impinge the culture, and to declare war on the formation of the culture that they did not understand. Because these invaders did not understand the nature of African culture, they tried to destroy African culture and replace it with their own. They were skillful in the management of their own culture, yet African culture in its manifestation was alien to them. And the crisis in Africa right now is a crisis of culture misunderstanding because nearly every state in Africa is ruled by an African trained in Europe; trained to discard his culture for an imitation of European culture that is at conflict with his own.

What we must do now is go back to the formation of the villages to study and understand African culture from a holistic view. It is apparent that they built enduring civilizations that lasted for thousands of years. Even before the foreigners had a jail system or a word in their vocabulary that meant jail, Africans had developed ways of doing things that still mystify the West to this day. With all the talk about who built the pyramids, and how they were built, there is no indication that there was a network of factories and yet Russia has a network of factories seventy-one years after the revolution that was going to change all mankind, and they don't have enough food to eat. There's something out of kilter here.

The one thing the African did because of his respect for nature, his respect for the seasons, his respect for the earth, and his respect for femininity as the giver of life was that he adjusted to the force of nature. The European on the other hand is still in defiance of nature. The African today who rules his country using European mythology has taken his people away from Africa, away from a concept of cultural rule that the African understands. He uses concepts that did not exist in Africa before. When you move the African away from Africa, his mind gets involved in some un-African things, and his conqueror or enslaver makes him think that their European things are universal and need protecting and legitimizing.

For example, just recently, the cause of Blacks was linked with the cause of gays. The ships brought no gays. They brought all men with their manhood, and women with their womanhood, and men who knew what to do with their manhood, with no confusion. When Nature or God or whoever you want to call it, designed man and woman, he purposefully designed them to go together. He did not design man to romance man. By design, there's not only a perfect fit with the lady, it is a glorious fit. It is something that should be approached with a certain degree of sacredness because if misused, it could be danger or disaster for both of them. The African took this all very seriously and approached it with a degree of sacredness in its own time and its own place. This is why you cannot compare the African attitude with the European attitude; they are coming from different cultural points of view. The European living in that varying climate and the Arab living in the sand made different uses of the female and developed a different attitude toward the female. Taken out of the African environment and placed in the European environment, you may develop the same traits and habits of the European without knowing that many of these traits are about as un-African as they can be.

We didn't bring wife beaters over here; we didn't bring men over here who made teenagers pregnant; we didn't bring any deserters; and women and men who created them. The people who are condemning us are making statistics and making themselves feel good pointing this out. They have created an atmosphere for their own existence, and by so doing have cut us off from natural outlets, natural job outlets, natural pleasure outlets, and natural intellectual outlets. The mind having to go somewhere, generally goes to the wrong place and instead of celebrating life, the mind begins to demean it.

My point (and I'm going to try to conclude so that you can ask some questions), is that we need to seriously reconsider where we are in the world. We need to seriously reconsider what role African people throughout the world have in coming back together, or whether we can even survive the results of this 500 year holocaust that is still very much active.

If people can make promises to you and break them, then it proves that you have been powerless for so long that you have forgotten the art of exercising power. It also proves that you misunderstand a major thing and that is education. Powerful people, never educate powerless people in the art and technique of how to take their power away from them. So to expect people to educate you, who cannot benefit by your education, is a condradiction in turn. They will train you to serve them, but they will not educate you because if you are truly educated, you will not ask for power; you will take it.

Now how does this relate to the subject? It relates very well because we cannot exercise power until we go back and celebrate life itself; until we recast religions; until we understand the nature of African culture; until we understand that instead of being a parasitic culture, ours is a protective culture. And, until we study the system among the Nors and learn that system was a forerunner of the fraternity and the sorority system that existed before the Greeks; until we throw away the Greek carbon copy and go back to the African original and rename our fraternities and sororities after African sororities and begin to assume African responsibilities and stop making it a social thing, we will continue to be subjugated. We must understand that organization is a celebration of responsibility and manhood is an assumption of responsibility. Maybe somewhere along our journey, We've taken a wrong turn at the fork of the road. Maybe we read the road signs wrong, and need to go back and re-read them. We've survived this 500-year holocaust, and have survived the fact that we have been under seige over three thousand years, one way or the other. Many people who were hit less than we were, are not on the earth any more because the blow took them away altogether. I'm saying that we must look at African celebration in a new way. When we begin to celebrate our survival on this earth in spite of the trials and tribulations, we realize faith has saved us for a special mission in this world. And I think it's a spiritual mission, a political mission, and a cultural mission in as much as our masters have worn out the carbon copy of their originality, if indeed they ever had any originality. They have copied from us and have made fortunes. What we need to do is to be more creative in using our own talent. We are a billion people on the face of this earth. Once we come together, and stop being consumers of everything and begin to produce something with our own effort, we can make ourselves free. Do you understand, that we can employ two-thirds of all the Black people on the face of the earth by furnishing goods and services to each other? If we ever achieve this kind of Pan American Nationalism as symbol of world unity that goes beyond Pan Africanism; if we begin to trade with each other, and if we begin to protect each other, the greatest celebration will be a celebration from dependency to true independence.

Moving toward this state of responsibility is our mission, because the achievement of this state is the legacy that we should leave for our children and their children still unborn. For, we would have celebrated life itself and by celebrating life itself we continue life indefinitely!

Thank you very much.

WHAT WILL WE TELL OUR YOUTH
ABOUT THEIR FUTURE?

We have a lot to explain and little time to explain it in. Dr. Ben and I are both veteran classroom teachers. We are accustomed to bells, so churches are not strange to us, and although we don't exactly belong to any churches, we do know something about time.

My topic that will be expanded on by Dr. Ben is a question: "What will we tell our children about our fight for freedom?" Further, "What will we tell our children about slavery, in general, about our slavery in particular?" What do we tell our children so they can stop turning their faces away, wanting to crawl under a table? When you mention our condition in the world, when will they stop blaming themselves? You have to know your oppressor and the nature of his oppression and what you would do about it. At what point, do we sit down and not argue about television? At what time do we sit down and tell simple stories about our revolutionary heritage, and get it across to our children that we have the longest revolu-

126

tionary heritage of any people on the face of the earth? We have fought longer and harder and against greater odds than any other people on the face of the earth. Why do our children not know this?

If our children knew of their true heritage and if they loved themselves, none of them would put poison in their veins. If they knew this, they would know that a code of conduct is expected of them, that they cannot afford to live selfishly, and that their conduct must reflect the best in a whole people. And when someone tried to lead them in ways not of their liking, they would have enough sense of their own selves to remember that we are not a people who engage in things of this nature; nor, are we a people who demean ourselves in this way.

But, for them to know this, they have to know what kind of society produced them -- that we come out of a collective society and are forced to live in an individual society. We think that we must take on the traits of our oppressor. Our role is to prepare to destroy our oppressor. His conduct in the world disgraces everything that could be called democratic and everything that could be called Christianity. It's even a disgrace to the things that mean the most to him like capitalism. He's misconducting himself in relationship to the one thing he used to try to hold onto in the world, which is the apparatus of exploitation.

Why can't we tell our children that whosoever God is, all people have the right and the responsibility to look at God through their own imagination and address God in a language of their own creativity? Why can't we calm ourselves down, then calm them down? What happened to the big kitchen where the family used to gather, to sip coffee or lemonade and begin to discuss matters pertaining to the family? And if the discussion became too delicate, we would send the children out to play and when the door closed, it was settled. The family, our Supreme Court, would have met and rendered a decision. We did not take the matter to the oppressor because we did not expect any mercy or understanding from him, in the first place. We handled it within the structure of the family. We don't do this anymore.

What are we going to tell our children about that period in human history, before the first European wore a shoe, or lived in a house with a window that we produced? What will we tell our children about that time when we did not have a word for jail because no one had ever gone to one; nor did we have a word for orphanage because no one had ever thrown away children. We also did not have a word for nursing homes or old people's homes because no one ever threw away grandpa and grandma. If we could fashion a society that had that much humanity, what can we do for ourselves today? And how can we explain the contradiction of a people, who could build the pyramids, yet can't maintain a candy store in Harlem?

A question came up in a meeting I was attending in Senegal from an errant member; one who I don't even know how he got there. He was in the midst of ethnic midstream, he didn't exactly belong to us, he didn't exactly not belong to us. He was what we call Hispanic and he said, "I have enough African blood to justify being here." But, he had no African loyalty. You must have African loyalty, having the blood is not enough because you have no commitment. And he kept asking his question very arrogantly and contemptuously saying, "Yes, you people built the pyramids; but, where are you now?" When I finally got tired of all his arrogance, I said, "Do we need them now? Let's build what we need right now." We need a railroad system stretching across Africa and we need to build it now. We need to have mining engineers and metal specialists to get the ore from the African earth. We do not need to buy the rails from outside; everything needs to come from inside of Africa itself. That's what we need right now. We need a road system of rapid transportation in Africa that would take a hundred years to complete. If we started this year we would have only ninety-nine more years to go. But, if you don't start it, you'll never know when it's going to be finished. We must, in this generation, start things that another generation will have to complete.

What are we going to tell our children about how we have survived away from home? What are we going to tell them about the circumstances in Europe and in the world, that caused them to be away from home? What are we going to tell them about the massive resistance movement in this country? What are we going to tell them about the most successful slave revolts we've had in the Americas, South America and in the Caribbean Islands? Not only what are we going to tell them, what are we going to tell the people of the Caribbean Islands who've seemed to have forgotten about it? At what point do we tell our children to stop wasting their time with Greek fraternities and sororities because all this nonsense and hazing, to get into a sorority and fraternity for which you have to literally humiliate yourself to get in, is not worth being a part of.

The African Secret Society, where the Greeks stole the idea in the first place, was one of responsible people. How do we get this point across to our people? And, how do we tell our children, whom we have sent to church, that while a European painted the picture up there, there is no proof that Christ really looked that way? We are not arbitrarily arguing against somebody else's depiction of him as being white. We just have to ask the question where was he born; was he a Greek or a Roman? First, we must remember that both the Greeks and the Romans were mixed. Then we can reason, if he wasn't Greek or Roman, the chances are he was one of those other people. And all those other people were non-white. So, we don't even have to argue about his shade. The main thing we have to establish is that he wasn't a Roman. Once that mention is made, I can walk away. I've finished my conversation.

What we have to do is stop wasting each other's time. I am not arguing against the church; I think the church should be an instrument of a people's liberation. In fact, everything that touches our lives should be an instrument of our liberation, and if it isn't, then it should be thrown into the trash can of history.

How do we explain ourselves to ourselves and then how do we explain ourselves to our children? When they read about slavery, we need to tell them yes, we were slaves, but this is what we did about it. These are the circumstances; these are the people who benefited from those circumstances; and, these are the people who are still benefiting from them. This is why we still have white slavery and why being Black is more severe on us. The greatest slavery is slavery of the mind, and every time you worship some degenerated bopper, or bee bopper, it is a form of slavery.

How do we tell people that because we are not dopes, we do not hang out with dopes? How do we tell them that we come from a society that is secure enough to accept the female as God, and that the people who feel insecure with the female in power are insecure as human beings. We had and still have a cultural lifestyle that makes a place for everyone in this society. Today, the woman plays an important role in the churches, behind the scenes and in the lodges. She is not taking power away from the man, she is freeing his hand so that he can be a better man.

Now where do we say we both went wrong? In reality, both Black men and women have gone wrong because we are looking at each other through the lens of Western Sociology invented to demean us. And we cannot, under any condition use it as a measurement. What are we going to tell our people about the unification of African people? What do we say that will help us achieve this kind of unification? How did we get lost on our way home? We need to meet again at the fork roads and read the road signs all over again. There are too many things that apply to our oppressor that do no apply to us. When we are longing to be like someone else, we allow ourselves to follow those who do not know where they are going. We need to set our own directions, instead of following people who have no direction. We are following a hungry and a very insecure people who want all of the world, but can't count halves, and who don't know a fourth, yet, want everything. They are of a personality bred by ice.

They are anti-democratic, and willing to achieve everything at the expense of sacrificing humanity, democracy and everything they called religion.

I have grown weary of trying to explain the difference between religion and spirituality because each time I make the argument someone says, "You must be godless." I am not godless. I am just trying to remove all of the unnecessary underbrush so that I can get closer to God, whomever he or she is. And, the "she" does not bother me either.

Now, let me pause and sum up something that has no summary and end something that has no ending. Where are we in the world, and how do we find ourselves and our place on the map of human geography? How do we tell people what went wrong? How do we get out of this terrible contradiction? After the independence of Ghana, we were so hopeful. We were in the midst of the Civil Rights Movement, the marches and the fight for a Caribbean Federation. We thought we had at last turned the corner on our way to true freedom and true unity. We underestimated our enemies, we also underestimated the members of our own group. Some of whom were our enemies. There were a whole lot of people who were not comfortable seeing African people in power. So between seeing and buying off a lot of them, the whole structure was lost.

The concept of a Caribbean Federation went by the wayside. The idea of total citizenship in this country also fell by the wayside. We were fighting for something that was a shadow; fighting for something the enemy could easily give us without losing its power. You want integration, so they give you integration. But, that won't give you money, jobs, or houses. So you can go to the same bathroom and eat at the same table. When you think of the prices these hotels charge, you could build five hotels with the money you spent going into their expensive hotels. By gaining integration you thought you didn't have to do anything for yourself. You still have to build your own. You still have to build an industry. There wouldn't be so many of our young people hung up in this stupid drama in the sand, had we not failed them by not making a place for them in our own community. Had we the funds, we could have opened up cloth factories, dress factories, shoe factories, all factories that deal with the things we use.

People get a little tired of my mentioning underwear because they are a little sensitive. But if one brother started manufacturing underwear and the rest of us said we are only going to buy from that brother, then he would become a multimillionaire on just that one item.

Now let's look at many items. We feed more than two billion dollars into the American economy. How can we use that money to rescue ourselves? With that kind of power, why are we still begging at the door of a fool? We want to locate ourselves on the map of human geography. There are millions of Africans in the Caribbean Islands, in the United States, parts of South America, and in the Pacific. There are over 150 million more in India and 500 million in Africa and the rest of the world.

We have taken care of some business well, while we have not done quite so well with other business. We will go into the 21st Century with a billion African people on the face of this earth. The idea is that we must not be a billion dependent people. We must not be a billion beggars. We cannot beg or steal for a piece of our own house. We have to straighten out our terminology. It wasn't about integration in the first place. Once you have justice and equality, then you can choose or not choose. There are a few Black people, including a few members of my family, that I'm not so hot on associating with, so they do not get invited to my home and I don't go to theirs. Likewise, I am not going to fall into the home of a white person, the minute integration is announced. I'm going to be just as selective about who I invite and whose invitation I accept.

My main point is that, our enemy has a program -- a well designed program. Our enemy has a mission and that mission is to control the world by any means necessary. If you are going to get him off of your back, you too must have a mission. You must have a priesthood, and you must go into the priesthood the same as someone going into a holy order. You must devote the rest of your life to making sure that your people have the basic necessities of life and more. We should get closer to ourselves, closer to our children, closer to the family structure. We have lived with these fragments for many years. Put them back together again, at least in a civil tone of voice. We have so much pent-up anger, with the real cause of that anger being racism and white oppression.

There are white people who manifest the same pent-up anger. Some people in Germany allegedly killed six million in a gas chamber. These people are willing to fight everybody except the Germans. They fight the Arabs, fight the Africans, anybody that's "we." We didn't put people into ovens, we know what to do with ovens. We are known for apple cobbler, deep dish apple pie, good roasts, good stews. We'll fix you a dish that will let you know that we invented cooking. We don't cook people, and don't have time to burn up people.

What I'm trying to say in the final analysis is that we must take control of ourselves. We must also realize that we have a continent that is 12 million square miles and that wherever our body may be on this earth, our cultural and political heart beat is in Africa. Whether you ever go to Africa or not, that is your home, that is the home of your spirit and that is the heart, meaning and definition of your commitment. None of us, in any place of the world, will be free until that continent is free. The tragedy of the continent is that Africans have lost their historical memory, as well as the time and the method they used when they were in charge of the state. Now every African state, with no exception, is an imitation of an European state.

I have found, much to my surprise, that the Africans in the Pacific have a healthier attitude toward African unity than those in Africa, the Caribbean and the United States. Whatever hit those people over there, hit them real hard because they are less polluted and less confused.

Any system in the world will work for you if you make it work for you. Any religion in the world can serve you, if you make it serve you. But a religion without spirituality is not worth your time, as religion in some cases has toned down the concept of spirituality.

We have to use the dictionary words right. Maybe we were fighting for the wrong thing. Maybe this whole concept of the United States of Africa is wrong in words. It sounds like an imitation. Why not a union of African states? Why not regional Pan Africanism that will feed into a continental Pan Africanism? Why not require language, and be conversant with at least one African culture? Shouldn't it be required to have some general knowledge of Africa as part of man's beginning on this earth? Instead of telling old English fairy tales, why not tell African fairy tales, or African teaching stories? And why not take genuine names other than Abdullah and Mohammed? You assume all these Arab names and think you're going African. Everybody in Africa who cannot be addressed as an African, is either an invader or a descendant of an African.

We must find ourselves on the map of human geography, and tell our children who they are. We must tell our children what their mission must be and the kind of legacy they have to leave for the whole world. We must also instruct them to begin with themselves in the essential selfishness of survival. That perception says, "Take care of yourself first, then find that mirror and see who's staring back at you." Use the word "we," and say, "We are going to change the world." If we gave the world humanity first, we will give the world the next humanity. And, as for getting ready for the job, we are ready to do it right now!

Thank you.

BOOKS BY JOHN HENRIK CLARKE

Rebellion in Rhyme (Poetry), The Dicker Press, Prairie City, IL., 1948. Reprinted: Africa World Press, Trenton, NJ, 1991

The Lives of Great African Chiefs, Pittsburgh Courier Publishing Company, 1958

History and Culture of Africa, Aevac, Inc. Educational Publishers, New York City, 1969

New Dimensions of African World History, Africa World Press, Trenton, NJ, 1990

African People At The Crossroads: Notes For An African World Revolution, Africa World Press, Trenton, NJ, 1991

African People in World History, Black Classic Press, Philadelphia, PA, 1991

PAMPHLETS

Black-White Alliances: A Historical Perspective, Third World Press, Chicago, IL, 1975

The State of the Race, Los Angeles Chapter, The Pan-African Secretariat, Los Angeles, CA, 1980

The End of the Age of Grandeur and the Beginning of the Slave Trade, Institute of Afro-American Affairs, New York University, NY, 1981

Thoughts on the African World at the Crossroads, N.E.R.A.C., Educational Pamphlet, Guyana, South America, 1980

FAMOUS SHORT STORIES

The Boy Who Painted Christ Black

Santa Claus was a white man

The Lying Bee

BOOKS EDITED

Harlem, A Community in Transition, Citadel Press, NY, 1964

Harlem, U.S.A., Seven Seas Publishers, Berlin Germany, 1965
Revised American Edition: Collier Books, NY, 1971

American Negro Short Stories (An Anthology), Hill & Wang, Inc., NY, 1966

William Styron's Nat Turner: Ten Black Writers Respond, Beacon Press, Boston, Mass, 1970

Malcolm X: The Man and His Times, MacMillan & Co., NY, 1969

Slavery and the Slave Trade, Edited with Vincent Harding, Holt, Rinehart & Winston, Inc. NY, 1970

Harlem: Voices From the Soul of Black America, New American Library, NY, 1970

Black Titan: W.E.B. DuBois, Edited with the Editors of Freedomways, Beacon Press, Boston, Mass., 1971

World's Great Men of Color, Vol. 1 & Vol. II by J. A. Rogers, (Revised and Updated with Commentary), Collier - MacMillan, Co., NY, 1972

Marcus Garvey and the Vision of Africa, Random House, NY, 1973

What's It All About, Edited with Vincent Harding, Holt, Rinehart & Winston, Inc., NY, 1969

Black Families in the American Economy, An E.C.C.A. Publication, Community Counselors Associates, Inc., Washington, DC, 1975

Paul Robeson: The Great Forerunner, Edited with the Editors of Freedomways Magazine, Dood, Mead & Co., NY, 1978

Pan-Africanism and the Liberation of Southern Africa: A Tribute to W.E.B. DuBois, United Nations Centre Against Apartheid and the African Heritage Studies Association, NY, 1978

Dimensions of the Struggle Against Apartheid: A Tribute to Paul Robeson, United Nations Centre Against Apartheid and the African Heritage Studies Association, NY, 1979

PHOTO CREDITS

1 - Mary Clarke Hobbs

2 - Mark W. Payne

3, 4, 5, 6 - Mary Clarke Hobbs

7,8,9 -Mark W. Payne

10, 11, 12, 13 - Barbara E. Adams

14, 15, 16, 17, 18, 19, 20, 21 - Claudia Joan Hurst

22 - Mark W. Payne

23 - Sybil Williams

24, 25 - Mark W. Payne

26 - Dr. Yosef Ben Jochannon

27 - Sybil Williams

28 - Mark W. Payne

29 - Kamau Davis

30, 31 - Allen Morgan

A MESSAGE FROM THE AUTHOR

Prof. Clarke retired from Hunter College in 1987, and has been busier than ever since leaving the classroom.

In 1991, he completed four books, which were published within the same year. Three of the books have been on the best seller list. During this same year, he lectured all over the country and abroad at least forty times, not counting his visit to Egypt. This visit to Egypt which was his fifth, was to celebrate the first African Nubian Festival. While in Egypt, Prof. Clark also lectured with Dr. Ben, his friend of forty years.

Earlier this year, overseas trips were made to Canada in February; followed by a visit to Japan where Prof. Clarke lectured to hundreds of troops stationed at the Yokota Air Base and Camp Zama in Zama; addressed the middle and high school students, and recited stories to the elementary and kindergarten grades. This trip, a high point of his career, was made possible by the cosponsorship of the Ebony Club of Zama together with donations and support from: the African-American Club, Atsugi; the African-American Club, Yokota Air Base; the Association of the U.S. Army, Japan Chapter; the Black Family Movement, Tokyo; Commander, 17th Area Support Group; Commander, U.S. Air Force, Yokota Air Base; Depot Community Organization; Director of Personnel and Community Activities; Dollars and Yen; Federally Employee Women; Japan Corps of Engineers, Civilian Welfare Fund; the Masonic Lodge, Sagamihara; Management and Staff of the Camp Zama Community Club; Noncommission Officers Association, 1140th Signal Bn.; Pride of the Orient Lodge #55, Camp Zama;the Retirees' Association; Zama Area Officers Wives Club; and the 500th Military Intelligence Association. The reception that Prof. Clarke received in Japan proves that he is everyone's favorite professor.

He received an honorary doctorate degree from the University of the District of Columbia, in Washington, D. C. on May 9, 1992.

This book, the first about Prof. Clarke's life, will hopefully set a precedent for a series of volumes to follow; and thanks to Prof. Clarke, with *The Early Years,* I was afforded an opportunity of a lifetime that I will always value and cherish.

AFTERWORD

"Until Africans throughout the world begin to tell their own story, the story will not be properly told." (John H. Clarke, *African World Revolution*).

CLARKE, The Early Years is a story about an African, properly told by an African. It is also a story about all Africans, particularly overseas Africans in exile and in search of their true identity and their cultural roots from which they have been dispossessed by the stories of other peoples.

To have known and worked with John Henrik Clarke for almost 30 years, is to have witnessed the fruition of the search that all Africans in the United States have consciously and/or unconsciously engaged in since the Americanization of the African. It is a fruition that now in Dr. Clarke's declining years is best manifested in a man at peace with himself and with the world, for he has found the answers to the questions that troubled the mind of the young cotton picker son of sharecroppers in anti-Black apartheid Alabama and Georgia.

John Henrik Clarke's search for his true self that Barbara Eleanor Adams artfully portrays is one that is unique to Africans brutally severed from their land and culture by the European slave trade. Its uniqueness derives as much, and perhaps more, from the psychological violence visited on those Africans who survived the "middle passage" to find themselves stripped of all physical and spiritual sustaining points of reference. The chattel slave environment in the United States was purposefully designed to reduce the African to a non-human piece of property. The past slavery Americanization process, however well meaning some may have intended and still perceive it to have been, in effect was and is but a means for legitimizing the cultural dispossession of a people.

CLARKE, The Early Years is the story of one African's triumphant victory over all of the historical forces set in motion to dehumanize a people. In that regard, it is a story of the struggle between the two souls that W. E. B. DuBois speaks of in his characterization of the Black man's search for identity in America. The message to overseas Africans of John Henrik Clarke's life, and achievements as a world renown scholar and teacher, is that only when Africans return to their own cultural roots will their true liberation be achieved. It is only then that Africa and Africans, wherever they are, will regain their rightful place in the history of the world.

To have known and worked with John Henrik Clarke has been an inspiration. The joy of reading *CLARKE, The Early Years* is to have recaptured the memories of a long personal and professional association with one of our intellectual heroes, and it is to know that the book was written by a former student and mentee, Barbara E. Adams.

Tilden J. LeMelle, Ph.D.
President
University of the District of Columbia